Proven SEO tactics

20 SEO tactics for the 2020's

Paul Haarman

I0472643

Table of Contents

About the author

My name is Paul Haarman, an online marketing consultant with a broad interest in online growth, SEO, online advertising and entrepreneurship. I studied Marketing at HEAO Business School and Business Economics at Erasmus University Rotterdam, The Netherlands. My company, Haarman Internet Marketing, is based in The Netherlands.

Since the last 17 years I am helping companies with their online growth. My main focus is SEO, online advertising, international growth and online entrepreneurship. I work as a consultant but I also make sure that some work is performed by myself as I believe that only by doing a job by yourself will gain the necessary insights that may help others to perform their job.

My customers come from all sorts of industries and are active in a myriad of markets. I work for small online entrepreneurs and for several multinational and Fortune 500 companies and everything in between. Although I work from The Netherlands, I live in Belgium and my customers operate in markets all over the world.
I believe in the power of the online world. We are living in such an exciting time frame that only in hindsight people will say "this was a defining period of our planet's history". We are in the midst of a transition process and if we understand its threats and embrace its opportunities this world can really become a better place.

The online world will evolve further, probably in a more human-centered dimension. The off line world will also reshape itself. During this process existing industries, markets and individual companies will undergo massive changes. We as a people will experience the same profound changes. What never will change are our human needs, our eagerness to learn and our drive to improve our individual and collective well-being. Optimization is one of the key characteristics of our human race. All inventions, all of society has come into existence through optimization. All progress is a process of learning and continuous improving. Sometimes the process goes slow, sometimes it speeds up as we experience the benefits. That is how the internet has come alive and conquered the world. That is also how we can work to improve our own business. It is also the case with online marketing. We need to optimize our performance day in, day out.

One step at a time, making the effort, doing our best. Of course that is also the way to improve our relationship with search engines. From the early years of the internet we have called it Search Engine Optimization as we all learned very quickly that driving organic traffic to a website is a matter of self-improvement by learning. It is not your search engine that should be optimized, it is you.

Paul Haarman, The Netherlands, 2019
Copyright © 2019 - 2020 Paul Haarman
Published by: Intellect Investments BV, Smederijstraat 2,
4814 DB BREDA, The Netherlands

Introduction

In my 15 years as an online marketing consultant and SEO specialist I have read so much about SEO that it would likely have overwhelmed me. But it didn't. Why? Because I decided to let the talkers do their talk and let the results speak for themselves. In search engine marketing there are 4 breeds of professionals: public speakers, trainers, writers and the ones that are actually optimizing search engine results for websites and online shops. I happen to be one of the latter species although I also train and write about SEO, but in that order.
It is the same thing with consulting work, you can only advise other people when you have the experience of doing the work yourself you are advising them to do. Of course that is an old-fashioned approach to work ethics. There are droves of successful coaches, consultants, event speakers and writers who excel in what they are doing: sowing the seeds of inspiration and motivation, providing food for thought. They only tell you what they have read or heard about what they are telling you but they do it in such a compelling way that you think it must be true. But when you are really into a specific topic, when you have experienced success and failures, when you have seen the results before your very eyes, only then you are able to separate the wheat from the chaff.
In the world of Search Engine Optimization there is a lot of talking and rumoring going on. This will get you to the top of Google, that will bring in traffic by the thousands, in 3 months you will rank number 1 on this keyword. SEO is sometimes presented as a magic key that may unlock the door to everlasting online bliss. There is a truth in that sentence. Yes, I believe Search Engine Optimization really is the key to online success, but it is not magic. On the contrary, SEO has nothing to do with magic, it is pure logic. That makes sense too as search engines are merely computers doing their sophisticated work in 0's and 1's.

Still, there are many empty promises uttered in the field of SEO. No, your website will not be number 1 on this high ranking keyword within 3 months. No, you cannot make a traffic magnet from a website without solid content using some sort of smart and fast SEO trick. There are no tricks, you will find none in this book that work.

So why this book? Because I think it is time to sum up the SEO tactics that really do work. How can I be so sure about what will work and what not? Sounds a bit presumptuous doesn't it? I agree, and that is not a label I like.

What I did is going through 15 years of SEO results. Going through Analytics accounts of hundreds of websites of many companies that are active in all sorts of markets. I have analyzed the inputs and outputs of SEO tactics for a myriad of websites, ecommerce sites, B2C platforms, B2B lead generating websites and non-profit websites. As online marketing is always evolving you will find only these tactics that work for the here and now and our online world of tomorrow. Explicitly I will mention these tactics that tap into new ways of using search engines. But you will also find some classic approaches that have performed and still are performing results. I have tried and tested all tactics I mention.

I put it all together to come up with a list of SEO tactics that generally work and I gave it a score on the impact these tactics had. I also came across tactics that didn't work. Some of them I performed myself and they worked in the past but they are obsolete now but still practiced by numerous SEO agencies. Some I encountered by customers that put them into place themselves (or by other SEO companies) and I could see the results, or rather the lack of them, while getting access to their website data.

So what you get here is a list of proven SEO tactics that will work. That is not the same as promising you that a certain tactic will always work instantly. Forget about instant success, but in many cases you will see results within a period of 2 months. There are ifs and buts of course. A completely new website on a fresh domain will have to wait longer depending on the competitiveness of the industry it is active in. A technical outdated website also will lag behind.

In all cases, Search Engine Optimization is a work of the mind that only comes to fruit after being implemented. That will cost you some blood, sweat and tears. Be aware of that. Nothing comes free and easy, I know that from my own experiences. Putting in time and energy is just hard work but when you see the results coming your way you know it was worth the effort.

In this book you will find the tactics explained and I will add the impact of this tactic by a score on stars (1 to 5 stars). But first I will explain why SEO should be on the top of your list in your online strategy.
Paul Haarman

The importance of SEO

If you manage a website or ecommerce site you will need to think about a lot of things. Of course it all begins with having a website that offers what you are selling whether that be tangible products, services, information, advertisements or whatever. Some people still believe that this is the most important part of online success, having a fine-looking, well-designed, state-of-the-art website that showcases your products or services in just the way you love it. As you are reading this book, you know they are wrong.

Online success has almost nothing to do with beautiful websites. It has everything to do with reaching the right target audience, getting them to enter your website, letting them interact with your website content, products and services and enticing them to act upon their aroused interest. Beauty is in the eye of the beholder, that certainly is true for websites and online shops. I have seen beautifully designed websites that did not bring in traffic nor interactions, let alone conversions. I have encountered websites that were incredibly outdated in design but highly effective in getting results.
That is not the same as saying that design doesn't matter. It does. An effective web design caters to the needs and expectations of your target market Sometimes beauty and effectiveness go hand in hand, sometimes it needs a more basic and practical design to convert traffic into leads and sales. The point I want to make is that you cannot look at a website and decide whether it is a great website or not. You will need to look a bit deeper. So I did.

What makes a website reach its goals?

I have gone through analytical data of hundreds of websites and ecommerce sites to detect the underlying powers of a website. After some years of digging through all these data I came up with 5 website value drivers that are responsible for the results and value of a website. Here they are:

The 5 website value drivers

1. Organic traffic strength
2. Online authority strength
3. Technical strength
4. Advertising & social strength
5. Conversion strength

In my book Website Valuation (sold on all Amazon shops) you will find a thorough analysis of these 5 website value drivers and a method of calculating the worth of a website. For this book it suffices to say that Organic Traffic Strength is the most important website value driver I discovered. Why is that? Because organic traffic is free, of high quality, often new to your site and enduring. Let us discuss its pros and cons a bit deeper. Cons I say? Yes there are, but nothing to be afraid of.

The pros of organic traffic

Of course we will begin with the positive side of organic traffic because it outshines the negative by far.

1. Organic traffic is free

Without traffic you can forget about online success. There are many ways to drive traffic to your website or online shop but most of them will cost you a handful of money. Online advertising may be very effective and if done properly it will turn in a positive return on your investment. But to keep it positive is a continuing challenge when competition is getting harder and advertising platforms ask more for the clicks they offer.
Social media without advertising on these platforms is becoming more and more difficult, especially when you are after some substantial traffic volume that does more within your site than a bounce back to where they came from.

There are not many options left that bring in free traffic that really is interested in your website. I dare to say that only organic traffic originating from search engines is the only reliable and solid option left. And free traffic is important, it may be essential to your survival as an online entrepreneur. In fact I know many online shops that would not be alive anymore if they did not get the free traffic coming from search engines like Google and Bing.
Even more importantly, the free traffic you attract may be the traffic paid for by your competitor. Especially when running an ecommerce site where margins are small your organic strength will keep newcomers at bay and the money you will save on the organic keywords may be put to use in paid keywords to broaden your market scope in areas where your organic authority is lower.
To put it simple: organic traffic that converts in leads or sales has by far the largest return on your investment compared to other paid sources.

2. Organic traffic is high quality traffic

No doubt about this. I found out that organic traffic is consistently number 1 or number 2 in conversions. Especially when you are looking at the combination of high conversion ratios and high conversion volumes it will almost always beat other traffic channels. What comes in second you might ask? In most cases Google Ads (if managed properly) and sometimes Direct Traffic, although Direct Traffic is also predominantly (branded) organic traffic.

When looking at other softer quality signals like bounce rate, time on site and pageviews, organic traffic is generally the top ranking channel. The reason for this is straightforward: organic traffic comes from a match between your website content and the search query of your visitor. When search engines do their job properly (and in most cases they do) your website content should be relevant to the search query.

3. Organic traffic is often new traffic

In most cases a significant part of your organic traffic consists of new traffic that did not visit your website earlier. In my analytical studies I found that generally organic traffic comes in second in attracting new visitors, after traffic generating from advertising channels such as Google Ads. I must make an exception however regarding branded keywords, especially keyword combinations that include the company name or exclusive brands offered. Here you will see a lot of existing traffic pouring in. But if you would exclude branded keywords, organic traffic attracts a lot of new visitors and this share rises still when large keyword combinations or long tail search queries are involved.

Why is attracting new traffic important? It will make the first interaction between a possible customer and your website content. New traffic is the corner stone for business growth. Even more importantly, new organic traffic tends to convert really well compared to other traffic channels. Looking at conversion ratios combined with conversion volumes it comes generally in second, after search engine advertising such as Google Ads. Why not first you might wonder? Well, search ads drive more buying oriented traffic as organic traffic is more information oriented.

4. Organic traffic tends to rise over time

Organic traffic is one of your most important website's engines. It will drive traffic to your site and it will keep on doing that even at a higher pace. Why is that? This is how it works:

A. **Excellent website content will be honored by search engines**
   Whenever you have published a webpage that gets right to the heart of the matter, search engines will notice its depth and thoroughness or its perfect answer to a question searched for. They will give it a high ranking because of that.

B. **Your audience will embrace your content**
   When visitors to your website also think your webpage offers just what they were looking for they tend to stay longer at your webpage and your website. They even might be tempted to perform the action you want them to perform (subscribe, get in touch or order).

C. **Search engines pick up the approval and interactions of your audience**
   Google knows when your audience likes your

website content. Time on page, time on site, bounce rates, conversions, all is noticed and stored. As search engines want to offer the best possible search results to their audience your splendid results will lead to even higher rankings or a steady place at the top of a search engine result page.

D. **Broader keywords will be given access to your webpage**
Whenever a webpage will be relevant on 1 or 2 search terms and it performs really well (in the eye of the Google's of the world) you will see that more slightly different search terms will be channeled to that same webpage.

Let's say your webpage has the perfect match for the search term "new Italian shoes for men". If the votes of your audience (time on page, time on site, high interactions) are favorable on that term you may see broader search terms coming to your webpage such as "Italian brown shoes for men" or "men's Italian brown shoes".

E. **The process may accelerate further**
If these broader search terms also perform well, if your website gains more authority, if other relevant pages on your website attracts these visitors the organic process will get in higher gear.
A lot of ifs of course, but you can help to get to this stage. That's the sport called Search Engine Optimization. And it is a sport, as there are winners and losers and very fine prizes to win.

The cons of organic traffic

Like I said, there are some minor issues with organic traffic that I need to discuss. These will not frighten you I think, but they are worth considering.

1. Organic traffic is not free

Well, the traffic is free but the road isn't. It's like riding a bike. Doesn't cost you a thing to get from A to B but you feel the sweat dripping from your back. And that bike you were riding on had to be bought and the road you were riding on had to be built. You know, nothing is for free in this world. Same with organic traffic.

What does it cost? A lot of time and energy to begin with if you would be doing things yourself. And that's the same as saying it will cost you money. Because it will be either your time and dedication or that of your employees or outside SEO consultant. Putting it in other words: Organic traffic is free but Search Engine Optimization is not. But that should not hold you back in investing time, energy and money. On the contrary, it is here that you can make the difference. SEO is a competing sport. You are investing your time and money to outperform the competition.

The greatest thing however is that it is not a question of putting in more time and money that will bring in results. It is all about doing the right thing that will make you an SEO winner. That is the purpose of this book, to avoid wasting time and money on things that do not work and to put all efforts in the things that make the difference.

2. Organic traffic cannot be targeted precisely

What do I mean? You can try to get in organic traffic around a specific theme but you cannot be sure to get in traffic on specific keywords. Some of you will frown now. Of course you can get in organic traffic on specific keywords you targeted in your SEO strategy. That is true, but you will not be sure that your website will get in organic traffic on specific keywords. In most cases you will get in relevant organic traffic on a broader base than the keyword you were looking for.

I myself will almost never target my SEO strategy on a specific keyword although I try to be relevant on the major keyword within that theme. An important reason for doing that is that I also want to get in Long Tail search queries surrounding that keyword but the point I want to make here is that SEO is not suited to pinpoint on specific keywords. In my opinion that is a drawback of organic traffic, it is not something you will have 100% control over. If you want your website to be visible on specific keywords, running a Google Ads or Bing Ads campaign makes more sense. In fact I love doing both, being active with SEO in a thematic way and precise targeting with search ads. It's like using a shotgun and a sniper rifle at the same time.

3. You cannot control the volume of organic traffic

This is a bit similar like the above mentioned point I made. If your SEO strategy runs well you will be getting more and more organic traffic. Sounds great but sometimes it may overwhelm you. You might say that it's a high class problem but there are situations that your organic growth and conversion growth do not match your company growth. I recall a situation with a customer who said to me that I generated a serious problem through my SEO work. Now my client had to decide upon hiring new employees. As this occurred in the middle of an economic downturn my client did not want to take the risk of hiring new personnel.

Another example: If you run an ecommerce site and you want to close down for a holiday it is easy to shut off your online advertising campaigns for a while. But organic traffic keeps pouring in. Of course you might choose to inform them about your absence and longer delivery times but this may cause some discontented customers.
It also works the other way around, you cannot tell up front what the growth in organic traffic volume will be while pursuing an SEO strategy. I often get this question: "What surge in organic volume may we expect after you have done your SEO work?". I can make some general expectations but that's the maximum I can do. Everyone who says otherwise hasn't been active in this fine line of business for long.

4. You are not behind the wheel

Your website may drive loads of organic traffic to your website but ultimately it is the search engine that is steering the traffic. If you have an active and sound SEO strategy in place you will be sitting in the passenger seat giving directions to your friendly driver. But if you fail to pursue a decent SEO strategy you are way back in the backseat crossing your fingers for a bit of luck (same feeling like some taxi rides I will never forget).
Is this a serious drawback? Well, it is just something you need to understand. You can push, pull, outsmart or cozy up to search engines in all sorts of ways, but you are never really in control. Like the old biblical proverb goes: Man proposes, God disposes. Not that search engines are somehow heavenly, but man, they come close.

But all things considered, organic traffic is a blessing

It really is, especially in this increasingly competitive online market place. As a somewhat seasoned online marketing consultant (I do this job for more than 15 years, pretty long in this line of business) I came across many online strategies that lead to tangible results. But having a solid SEO strategy that will get in a good chunk of organic traffic was and still is number 1 on my online marketing list. I have the data to prove it. It is true for B2C and B2B markets and it is the same for small, medium-sized and big websites with loads of traffic pouring in from all sorts of channels. Organic traffic beats them all on an input – output level (money or energy invested versus results).

But what is a solid SEO strategy?

There is not one road to organic traffic happiness but a choice of several roads to choose from. You have different SEO tactics to pursue but it depends on your website, your market and the SEO opportunities at hand what strategy will be the best to follow. So if you are looking for one single SEO plan that is suited for all websites in all markets I will have to disappoint you.
In general I will use different strategies for ecommerce sites and lead generating sites. I will use a more niche approach in highly competitive markets and I will use a different strategy for new websites compared to old website domains with already a vast influx of organic traffic. That being said, the strategy may vary, but the tactics I will choose from are known to me. What I mean is that I have a number of tactics at my disposal that I know they will perform. A solid SEO strategy consists of a number of SEO tactics that will suit the given situation best.

The right choice of tactics makes the right strategy. The main question addressed in this book is: What SEO tactics really do work? That will create the toolbox to choose from.

In the next chapters you will find 20 SEO tactics that work. Is this general knowledge? Not at all, there is much debate going on between search engine specialists what tactics work best. Are there more effective SEO tactics out there that you do not find in this book? Probably, I can only tell you my experiences, there is room for another book like this by someone else.

These are my personal findings but they are a bit more than that. All tactics described in this book I have witnessed with my own eyes. I have gone through hundreds of Analytics data from as many websites, ecommerce sites, lead generating sites, company websites and online platforms and I have seen their impact. Every single SEO tactic I have measured according to their results. So what do you get? You will learn the tactics that have a proven result in driving organic traffic. I will also add the impact strength of each tactic varying from 1 star (a minor result) to 5 stars (major results).

The impacts on results are general impacts calculated for all sorts of websites. Some tactics give better results for different websites and markets so you will get the aggregate result. Again, each website and market deserves a specific SEO strategy, consisting of a couple of these tactics. But choosing between a bunch of good apples always makes a better apple pie than mixing it with rotten ones. A good SEO strategy is 100% depended upon good tactics.

20 SEO tactics that really work for the coming years

On the next pages you will find 20 SEO tactics for the 2020's. As I said before, these are all proven SEO tactics. What does that mean "proven SEO tactics"? Well, exactly what it sounds like. They generate measured results in gaining extra organic traffic after they have been implemented.

These tactics are not proven by the SEO specialists you may encounter through numerous SEO blogs out there. They are proven by statistics I have found myself in hundreds of analytical data I scrutinized from websites I have worked with. Mind, I love many SEO blogs and I am sure that some of the SEO tactics I describe here you may also have encountered while searching the internet. That is not an issue for me, I just want to see with my own eyes if a tactic works or not. Call it stubbornness if you like. With every SEO tactic that works I add an impact in 1 to 5 stars. 1 star means a minor impact, 5 stars a huge impact.

Talking about impact, what do I mean by that? There are absolute impacts, relative impacts, swiftness impacts and durability impacts. An absolute impact would be a rise in organic traffic by 1.000 visitors a month. A relative impact would be a rise of organic traffic with 20% and a swiftness impact would be the number of weeks or months it takes when the impact will kick in. The durability impact will say something about how long the impact of the SEO tactic will last, will it give a short spike in traffic and then fade away or will it gain momentum in time? To make things a bit more confusing, the impact of a specific SEO tactic also depends on the website, its already established online authority, the seniority of its domain, the technical condition of the website and SEO works already performed. How to calculate impact in such a multi-dimensional SEO environment?

What I did is taking score of SEO impacts of all sorts of tactics from all sorts of websites and ecommerce sites. The result was of course some kind of hotchpotch of impacts, minor ones, huge ones, high and low relative impacts, short and long durability impacts and so forth. That was one part of the job. The second part was adding all impacts of each different SEO tactic, small and large and calculating their average impacts. At the end this exercise provided me a thorough insight in the impact each SEO tactic had in driving extra organic traffic.
So what do you get from all this? In the next chapters you will get an overview of all SEO tactics I investigated during the last 5 years.

In the following pages you will learn the SEO tactics that really made an impact. I will also go into some well-known tactics that really did not work. I will showcase them in a rather random way. That is a conscious choice of mine. Otherwise you might think that the highest impact scores are the ones you would need to execute. But all these tactics with rather small impacts may just make the difference between a good and a great SEO result.

1] Old-fashioned hierarchy

Total average SEO impact: ★★★★★

Search engines need your help

Search engines do not give a heck about egalitarianism. They are truly old-fashioned in their way of thinking. But forgive them, it is in their DNA. They are built to rank and make order from chaos. They do that by constantly making decisions upon more or less important. They do not hide this character trait, it is the essence of what they do, listing up search results from 1 to a zillion based upon relevance and importance. So it should not come as a surprise that they use this line of thinking in all their daily work. But they too are overwhelmed by the load of disorder and non-structural content we throw at them. Believe me, being a search engine is a tedious and exhausting job. They have headaches all the time. So please, give them a helping hand. They really do appreciate it. If they crave for order and ranking we can help them making their lives easier by supplying them with a hierarchical URL structure. They are looking for logic, let's give it to them. They will pay you back,... big time! Let me explain what I mean by using a hierarchical URL structure.

What is a hierarchical URL structure?

A hierarchical URL structure links relevant webpages to each other in a logical and hierarchical way. The concept of hierarchy is based upon the notion of superiority. Sounds discriminatory and in a way that is exactly what it is. In a hierarchical URL structure we will place a relevant but subordinate webpage under the more superior webpage. In most cases you can translate that into putting a more specific webpage under a more broader thematic webpage.

Let us examine some hierarchical URL's.

www.example.com/shoes/mens-shoes/mens-sneakers

This is a hierarchical URL that puts Men's Sneakers under Men's Shoes and the webpage Shoes is the most superior, or better said, broader webpage.

So the more specific webpages are lying under the more broader webpages. Why is that important? Search engines are very clever, they can discern good content from bad content, they can distinguish a fine sentence from a spammy one but they also welcome some help in their work. By linking webpages to each other via a logic URL structure they will understand your website content better and faster. By adding a hierarchy to the URL structure they will learn that your website offers depth within a specific theme.

In the example above search engines understand that your website offers more than only shoes, it offers men's shoes and on an even deeper level they will find men's sneakers. If you would not link these 3 webpages to each other, search engines would find separate pages without the connection of relevance.

Do never forget: search engines may be very clever, and they are, but in essence they are machines we call computers. They thrive on logic, they love math and they need help from our human beings. Let us support them! What do you gain by using a hierarchical URL structure? More organic traffic, yes. But from which pages? Let us go back at our example:

www.example.com/shoes/mens-shoes/mens-sneakers

This is one webpage that will get you to the men's sneakers page on your website. Will this page become more relevant for search engines or will the upper levels bring in the traffic?

So these are the 3 webpages:

www.example.com/shoes
www.example.com/shoes/mens-shoes
www.example.com/shoes/mens-shoes/mens-sneakers

You may have read that a higher level URL is theoretically more important to search engines than a lower level URL. So in theory the page www.example.com/shoes should be driving more organic traffic than the webpage www.example.com/shoes/mens-shoes/mens-sneakers.

But in practice that is not the case. Well, in theory it isn't either. A higher level URL is higher in hierarchy, not in relevance. I noticed that from my research. What happens when you put new webpages in your website using a hierarchical URL structure? Within 1 or 2 months you will generally see the most specific webpage (the lowest level in hierarchy) begin to pick up organic traffic. After a few months you will see the higher level URL's driving more and more traffic. So it works the other way around. There is a lot of logic into that of course. Search engine optimization is all about relevance and you will find that more on specific lower level pages than broader higher level pages.

What a hierarchical URL structure really does is linking a specific relevant page to broader themed but relevant webpages. So you will add some thematic juice to the more specific webpage by bringing this page under the banner of relevant thematic webpages. Your gain is threefold:

1. Your more specific webpage will be better understood by search engines and it will get in organic traffic faster and in higher volumes.

2. The upper level webpages become more relevant as you are providing depth by linking it to a deeper level more specific webpage. So your upper level webpages become more relevant.

3. Your website as a whole gains in relevance as search engines will know at a glance what general themes your website offers. So in our example your website will gain importance and relevance on the very broad theme of shoes and men's shoes by using a hierarchical URL structure, but of course you will need more than 1 string of webpages to do that.

Another thing to take into account: With ecommerce sites that use a hierarchical URL structure on their product pages (like the example above with shoes) you will provide relevance and logic to search engines but this will not suffice to boost your organic traffic. There is so much competition from other ecommerce sites that will use more or less the same hierarchy and even more or less the same website content (same brands, same product details) that you will need to act upon it from a different angle. It still is wise to use URL hierarchy on your ecommerce pages.

But for a real SEO boost you might consider the following content approach:
www.example.com/buying-tips-shoes/buying-mens-shoes/how-to-buy-mens-sneakers

Now you can use original website content within a hierarchical URL structure. That is the combination you are looking for.

So, what to do?

- Think in themes and subthemes.
- Put the broader theme on a higher level of hierarchy than the smaller theme.
- Link from a higher hierarchy page to a lower one.
- Write about your products instead of only showcasing them (as in an online shop environment).
- Combine relevant keywords in one hierarchical URL structure, make another URL hierarchy form less related themes or keywords.

Most important

Make sure you name your URL's congruously with your URL hierarchy structure.

2] I love Brandon Baseball Cards

Total average SEO impact: ★★★★

Use the Brandon Baseball Cards keyword URL structure

Keywords in URL's are a no-brainer you might say. But it is not so straightforward as one would think.

Some questions pop to mind:

1. What keywords to use in your URL?
2. And what about repeating keywords in URL structures?
3. Is there a logical strategy to follow in establishing URL's?

To begin with the last question, there is. I call it the Brandon Baseball Cards URL structure. Eh, what? Let me explain. Back in the old ages of the internet (I think it was around 2006 or 2007) Google came up with a starter guide for Search Engine Optimization. Initially this document was made for internal use by Google. It was aimed at Google employees that were active in Google's Search Department to cover the basics how SEO worked in line with their own search engine. After a while they decided to publish this document for webmasters to help them in their SEO strategy. It was one of the very few times that Google came up with real insights about what would work and what to avoid.

The official name of the document is called Search Engine Optimization Starter Guide and although Google has cut the link to this document it is still available through some other websites. While reading you will not find a lot of thrilling stuff, it is all very basic but that doesn't make it less valuable. There is one part however where Google explains how to make up URL's which is the jewel of this document. They use an example of a fictitious website that sells baseball cards under the name of Brandon Baseball Cards and this has always been the name that stuck in my mind.

In one of the examples they use the following URL: http://www.brandonbaseballcards.com/articles/ten-rarest-baseball-cards.htm

Remember, this was in the days way before HTTPS was being used.

Within this document Google explains that using a logical and descriptive (readable) URL structure improves the usability for users and search engines. Search engines inform themselves by these descriptive URL's. In Google's own words: "If your URL contains relevant words, this provides users and search engines with more information about the page than an ID or oddly named parameter would".

When reading Google's document and looking at the URL structure you will notice that using a keyword within the URL is fine by Google and even more importantly they advise to repeat it in lower levels of the structure.
I have expanded the Brandon Baseball Card concept and I found out that as long as your URL is adding depth to the central keyword you may use the central keyword within that lower level URL.

In practice this would be a SEO friendly and correct URL:

www.example.com/used-cars/used-cars-ford/used-cars-ford-mustang

It may look spammy but it is not as with each deeper level page you will add depth to the central keyword "used cars". I used this keyword approach in URL structures very often and the results are great.
Coming back to this Brandon Baseball Cards concept, is it still valid after all these years? Yes, it is and the same goes for almost everything that is included in this Google document. You might say that it is the core of SEO, so please do read it.

Answering our first question, what keywords should you choose in your URL? It depends on your webpage content and the central theme or subtheme that you are aiming at. But the structure must always be logical and the URL naming should reflect the webpage content.

So, what to do?

- Start with identifying relevant keywords.
- Group keywords together in a URL structure and repeat the central keyword theme.
- Make sure your content perfectly matches the URL.

Most important

Repeat keywords in your URL, but always add depth.

3] A simple hyphen makes sense

Total average SEO impact: ★★★

Use hyphens in URL's and domains

This is all about the proper use of URL's. This one was a bit hard to measure as I had to compare the impact between different kinds of websites but I dare claiming it valid. Besides, Google backs me up on this one as they also stress the importance of using hyphens when a keyword consists of 2 or more separate words.
What are we talking about? It is all about making a decision on how to use words in domains in URL's. Many keywords, brands or company names consist of more than 1 word. The central question is here how you can help search engines understanding the words you use in domains and URL's. Let's say you have an ecommerce site that sells mountain bikes. Your company name is Johnson Mountain Bikes and you also sell the more expensive carbon frame mountain bikes. What domain and URL will be better and faster understood by search engines, 1 or 2?

1. www.johnsonmountainbikes/mountainbikes/carbon mountainbikes

2. www.johnson-mountain-bikes/mountain-bikes/carbon-mountain-bikes

Well, search engines are almost human. The second one wins, hands down, we can read it better and so do search engines.

If you are searching the internet you will notice that most companies do not use hyphens within their domain name. With company names this is not a big problem but if you would want to register or buy a keyword domain name then picking the one with hyphens is your best option. So the first one is better than the second one:

1. www.buy-shoes-online-4-me.com

2. www.buyshoesonline4me.com

All the same, keyword domains are a relic from the past. It is not your domain name that matters, it is your URL structure.

Another thing to keep in mind: Use only hyphens to distinguish between one word or another within your URL. Forget underscores or capital letters, they do not function the way hyphens do.

So, what to do?

- Always use hyphens as a separator in URL's.
- If possible use a hyphen in your domain if a keyword is involved.

Most important

Hyphens are extremely more important in your URL structure than in your domain name.

4] Forget English

Total average SEO impact: ★★★★★

Use the language of your target audience

Oh, this is so important. Sounds obvious you might think but I come across so many websites that ignore this simple and basic rule.

The rule is simple and clear:

1. Use the language of your target audience in website content, URL's, image descriptions (often overlooked)

2. If you have a worldwide audience you might want to select only a handful of large languages but do not expect that you will attract much traffic of all these smaller countries with distinctive languages

3. Use the domain extension of each important country if possible. If this is not feasible use a multi lingual website on a generic domain (preferably a dot-com)

Never use English to appear worldly

When you are living in an English speaking country you will not encounter this problem. But in all those other countries where English is not the main language it is a mistake often made. Of course it makes perfect sense to operate a multi-language website. That is not what I address here. The issue here is that some websites based in a non-English spoken country only use English on their websites. They do not use the native language but their target market is in most cases their own country or a mix of national and international customers.

The problem is most common in smaller countries that have their own native language. They build websites in the English language as they think that their customers also speak English. I see it in countries like Belgium, The Netherlands, Sweden, Norway, Denmark and Finland. These are all countries with an open mind and eagerness in doing business abroad. You will not find it much in larger countries like Germany, France, Spain or Italy. In these countries the native language is perceived as more important.

Why do some companies choose English as their only website language?

1. They think that the English language will give them a more international and worldly appearance

2. They are used in speaking English (like some international companies or accountancy firms)

3. They think that their target market will speak English and search the internet in English

Whatever the reason: Stop doing this! Make a multi lingual website or use different websites in different languages but always use your own native language when your target market is your own country.

So, what to do?

- Write in the language of your target audience.
- Use English when you target an English speaking audience.
- Use English when you target an international audience and your budget does not allow for using native languages for all countries (but do not expect to see great results).

Most important

Never use English to appear mundane.

5] Use country specific domains

Total average SEO impact: ★★★★

When you are targeting a country the best option is to use that country specific domain. So if your target market is France your best choice would be www.example.fr.

Why is this?

Search engines and especially Google give priority to websites with domain extensions catered to a specific country. This has everything to do with providing the most relevant search results to local users.

In recent years this has become more and more the standard approach of search engines. Since early 2018 Google has even stepped up local relevance by supplying the bulk of search results that match the country you are logged into with your Google account. The reason behind this strategy is a further local oriented roll out of Search Engine Result Pages which also allows for tapping into local advertisers. It is becoming more and more expensive to advertise with Google Ads nationwide as local players may afford higher bids as they are more likely to get higher conversions or they are able to spend an affordable budget to their specific local market taking for granted a higher CPC. So it is in the interest of search engines like Bing and Google to further segment local markets.

I will give you an example of my own. I am a Dutch citizen but I live over the border in Belgium. As we speak the same language (Dutch) in this part of Belgium and The Netherlands I am used to visit more websites originating from The Netherlands where there is a much larger offer of all sorts of websites in all possible industries (especially in ecommerce). Since the beginning of 2018 this abruptly changed as from then on almost 80% of search results had a dot-BE (Belgium) extension instead of a dot-NL (Netherlands) extension.

So what will be your best choice?

If you want to target a specific country use the country specific domain or country code Top Level domain (ccTLD) as it is properly called. This is simple when you are living in the country you service. You just pick the extension of your country for your domain. Do not fall for the temptation of using a sexy dot-com domain even if it is free. You may want to register it (always a good advice when your brand may grow to international proportions) but from an SEO viewpoint you must not use it within your country, except when you are living in the USA.
Adding to that, the dot-com extension is generally used in the States but in fact it is not the proper country specific domain, that is the dot-USs extension. For some reasons dot-com has won the battle over dot-US within the States (many reasons I will not bother you with). Search engines adjusted for that and they treat a dot-com as a proper country specific extension for the United Sates although it is in fact a generic Top Level Domain (gTLD).

But what to do when expanding internationally?

Should you build individual websites on country code Top Level Domains or use a generic one? Let me be VERY clear about this: your best option, SEO-wise, will be using different ccTLD's for each and every country you are targeting. That means different websites to manage, different hosting services and maybe a bit more headaches and costs. From an SEO point of view however this is absolutely your best option. One added advantage will be that this also gives you the option to host each different country specific domain within the country you are targeting which will have a positive impact on loading speed for your target audience (and this speed also has a positive impact on search engine rankings). Looking at it from an organizational or time saving and cost consciousness point of view you might want to opt for a generic Top Level Domain such as a dot-com, a dot-org or a dot-net (or dot-shop, dot-hotel etc.). Then you will be using a multi lingual website.

Using a language denominator

You may address language issues by adding a language denominator to your generic extension. This will look as: www.example.com/fr

There is some confusion about using language denominators. Search engines do understand it so that's fine but you are not addressing a country with it, it is aimed at the language. So in the above mentioned example search engines do not understand whether you are targeting France, Canada, Switzerland or Senegal. You cannot do that with language denominators. I have seen problems arising from this approach especially with companies that offer different products, services and prices for different countries. Search queries in French popped up in many French speaking countries where it wasn't intended because of different market approaches. But all in all you might want to opt for a multi lingual website solution even if you know it is not optimal.

Using subdomains

Another option would be using subdomains to address different countries like: www.uk.example.com (for the United Kingdom). The positive part of using subdomains to cover different countries is that it will distinguish the different countries in your market approach, the negative is that each subdomain is treated as a different entity to rank on. So if your USA subdomain is doing great it will not help your UK subdomain in building organic authority. This may be a minus, especially when dealing with different subdomains for the same language (such as the UK and USA). If however prices and conditions will be different between let's say the UK and the USA this may be just what you are looking for. In distinguishing between different countries and languages the use of subdomains may be the right choice in most cases.

So www.fr.example.com will not cause language confusion on the part of search engines with the subdomain www.usa.example.com. However there is one single drawback of using subdomains: As country code TLD's target countries, and the language denominator within URL's covers different languages, subdomains will not add specific country relevance to your SEO strategy. What it will do is illuminate confusion for your own organization and target audience.

So what to do?

- ccTLD's are the perfect approach in targeting different countries.
- The language denominator within URL's does not add organic strength for different countries, use it in multi-lingual websites.
- Subdomains may look logic and will separate different markets for your audience and own organization but they do not add extra country specific organic strength.

Most important

Take time to think it over. The decision about domain extensions is an important one that is not easily to be reversed when things are set in motion.

6] Put some sense in your header tags

Total average SEO impact: ★★★

Structure your header tags

What are we talking about? First let me quickly explain what headers are. They are the titles of your page or paragraphs within your article or webpage. Header tags are HTML codes to describe these headers. You probably heard of H1 and H2 headers, these are HTML tagged headers.

An H1 header tag looks like <h1> </h1>. This H1 header tag is reserved for the main title of your webpage. If your main title would be: **10 things you need to do to survive a plane crash** it would be tagged like this:
<h1> 10 things you need to do to survive a plane crash </h1>

The optical result would be a large title in bold looking like this:
10 things you need to do to survive a plane crash

The HTML result will be that search engines will understand that you have designated this to be the main title of your article or webpage.

H2 and lower ranked H3 and H4 header tags work similarly. In essence an H1 header tag has more authority than an H2 or H3 header tag. The main title of a webpage will be stored as more important than a paragraph title which all makes sense. Search engines use header tags to understand what your webpage is all about so a proper use of header tags will teach search engines fast

What do I mean with structuring these header tags? Search engines love structure, they are machines however clever they are and they are programmed in a logical order. That does not impede them to learn by themselves but their foundation is purely logical. This also impacts the use of header tags. In my research I compared different types of webpages in the use of header tags. This is what I found:

1. Use only 1 H1 header

This makes perfect sense. There is only one title of a webpage. So please, do not make the mistake in addressing more H1 headers to one webpage. Is it important? Yes, search engines will be confused otherwise, their first task is to understand what your webpage is all about. One H1 header will help them, no H1 header will leave them in the dark, more H1 headers will confuse them.

2. Use several H2 headers

There is no limit in H2 headers you may use. In fact the more, the better. But, be sure that each H2 header or paragraph header will reflect a specific in depth part of the total webpage. In other words, H2 headers should be followed by copy. It may be 2 or 3 sentences but preferably more than 10.

3. Use H3 headers to further specify or sum up

Most important: always use an H3 header below an H2 header. So do not put an H3 directly under an H1 (or an H3 under an H4). Just always follow the structural order going from more important to less important. What you may do however (and I explicitly recommend it) is to put an H2 under an H3 header. That is what you do when you start another paragraph after you have finished the previous paragraph.
How to use H3 headers? I use them a lot for summing up features or give in depth specifications within a particular paragraph.

4. H4 headers and below, you may forget about them

As a header these lower order headers do not add much to the structure of your webpage. I myself do not use them much. What they may do is adding extra depth and structure to a large article. But in most webpages I prefer to stick to H1, H2 and H3 headers. In comparing results I cannot make the case for using these lower header tags as I can do for using H2 and H3 headers.

5. Use at least 5 H2 headers

Search engines prefer webpages with an in-depth description of the central theme. I found that pages with more than 5 H2 headers do perform better in general in triggering organic traffic. A long article with no H2 paragraph headers hampers transmitting structural information to search engines. So, please use H2 headers. In writing an article it helps to think in paragraphs. It will generate more ideas about webpage content and it also entices a structural approach in writing.

6. Make sure that your H1 header consists of the central theme keyword

The central theme keyword (or better keyword combination) is NOT the central theme of your website. It is the central theme of your webpage. So if you are running a website in skincare products your website central theme will be "skin care". The central theme of a single webpage may be "skin care for women over 50". Always think first about what you are going to write about. That will be your H1. All subsequent headers and paragraphs should be about digging into this central theme further and further.

So, what to do?

- Use header tags in a logical way.
- Concentrate on your H1 and H2 headers.

- Your H1 header does not have to be the same as your URL, it may be longer but make sure a central keyword is included.

Most important

If your font size is too large do not use a lower header. Alter this header in your template or CMS to the font size you want.

7] King of local search

Total average SEO impact: ★★★

How to build local relevancy?

If your service area is regional, local SEO will be on top of your list. Unfortunately local SEO is one of the toughest parts of our distinguished science. Why is that? Main reason is that many ways of claiming local relevance may interfere with the way how search engines go about it. Of course your physical address will substantiate your local relevance if this address is situated within the locality you want to be found for. But I guess that there are more competitors like yours that also have their physical address in the same town or region so your physical address alone will not do the trick.

What can you do? Adding the names of places and regions to most of your website content? Sounds desperate and that's just the way search engines will view it. Never forget, hard manipulation doesn't work, neither in life nor on the internet. And soft manipulation isn't manipulative, it is being helpful (hmm, well, if it's not executed by politicians).

But what does work in local SEO?

The first rule to think about is the following: You cannot be relevant on all themes with SEO. That is the problem with online shops that offer a very broad mix of products. They are never as relevant as a specialist store (although the high traffic volumes of some online platforms will help them). In general though, you must take sides. You must pinpoint the themes you want to be relevant for. That is most certainly true for local SEO. You cannot be regionally relevant for both New York and Los Angeles or for both Poland and Italy without the regional relevance supporting it. Think of taxi companies that want to be relevant on all possible cities and villages or lead generating sites that want to tap into local search traffic. That doesn't work (anymore I must add, because in the past you could get away with it and even now it sporadically will work). So what to do? Here are some useful tips:

1. Choose the region you want to target

The smaller the region, the more specific your local area, the better your chances will be to become the local search king (or queen of course). If 80% of your business comes from 1 area do not go for the other 20%. Never forget: In the end the volume of organic traffic does not matter, it is conversions we're after. Do not chase for high flying birds when ducks are walking around your feet (is that a saying? Well now it is).

2. Focus on your complete website

Local SEO is not a thing you manage on webpage level alone. This is a big difference with most other SEO strategies where you may be relevant with one webpage on one theme and with another webpage on another theme. With local SEO your strategy must consist of a holistic approach. Your targeted location(s) should radiate from every single webpage in your website.

3. Show the link to your targeted region

This is the 1 million dollar question of course. Why are you relevant for this geographical region? Is it because your business is situated there? Is it because you ONLY service this area? So tell them! But, make sure that you tell the truth. Make it logic. Explain why you are servicing this area. Maybe you will not calculate call-out fees serving this area, maybe your shop has only 1 physical location where people need to come to. Just make sure that your local relevancy is understood by your target audience, your search engine will follow.

4. Get locally involved

Supporting a local sports club, sponsoring the annual fair, donating to your local charity, it all makes sense if your target market is local. And spread the word out of course!

5. Occasionally blogging about local matters

No harm in blogging (although in many cases blogging is not the best SEO strategy). Blogposts should be about actual things, things that matter more now than tomorrow. That may perfectly fit in with a local SEO strategy. Make the local link in your blogpost. Write about your area and combine it with your proposition and website theme.

And what if you're not a local player?

Like I said before, do not try to pretend local if you're not. But that isn't the same as telling that you are not allowed to claim local relevancy being a national or even global player. You still can do that if your claim makes sense. So first you have to look for logic in your claim.

Here are some local relevant situations for non-local players:

- **You have local reference projects you may showcase**
  Why not? Cluster all your reference projects into local reference pages (including local URL's and local headers) and focus on local relevance. Your local reference page may look like:
  www.example.com/us-office-building-projects/new-york-office-building-projects
  Of course, building content around such pages adds more flavor to it all. Do not stop by putting up only photographs and small copy, expand on it!

- **You have local representation you may highlight**
  Nothing wrong with that! If you are a regional, national or even global player you still may be locally relevant based upon your local representations. This may be a company outlet, a local distributor, a sales representative or even an agent. What's important is how you handle it. My advice: reach out to your local representative and showcase its business. Include interviews with local representatives, talk about local projects and let this local sauce drip all over your page(s).

- **You have solved some local problems you may want to share**
  Whatever your business is doing, you will have customers that paid for your products or services to help solve their problems. When you are a plumber you may have helped some customers just outside your hometown. When you are a building company you may have helped rebuilding homes after a hurricane in another state. Maybe you can share a wonderful story about helping a customer in another town. Just share it with us! We will love to hear it, as long as it is authentic, original … and true of course!

And what if you cannot claim some local relevancy?

Just stop acting as if you are a local. We can hear it from your accent. You are not born here, I bet you were never here before. Go back where you came from! Well, search engines may sometimes behave a bit rude. No law against it, yet.

So, what to do?

- Add local relevancy to your content.
- Think of local stuff you can add in an original and authentic way like reference projects, local agents or local representations.

Most important

Do not overdo it, you cannot claim local relevancy when there is no basis for it.

8] We'll have to talk

Total average SEO impact: ★★★★★

Tap into conversational searches

Conversational searches are getting increasingly important. People are changing the way they use search engines. It is getting more personal and with the advent of voice search I am 100% convinced that conversational searches will become the challenge of SEO specialists and search engines. Because that is what they are, both challenges and huge opportunities. But let us start by explaining what they are.

Conversational searches are search queries that treat search engines as trusted personal advisors. These search queries are direct questions on a personal level. In most cases they begin with "Can I", "Should I" or "Do I need". In a recent study by Google it showed that search queries beginning with "Should I" and "Do I need" see a 65% growth annually. "Can I" searches even grow at a rate of 85%.
These conversational searches replace more utilitarian searches that include only the basic keywords. What's happening is that we are treating search engines more as help providing intimate friends instead of computers that are just performing a task.

Examples utilitarian versus conversational searches

Here are some examples of what we used to type into search bars and how we are treating them today (and especially tomorrow):

"best anti-aging skin care" becomes "what anti-aging skin care do I need?"

"tickets available Carrie Underwood" becomes "can I get tickets for Carrie Underwood?"

"tyres Ford F-Series" becomes "which tyres should I buy Ford F-Series?

Mobile and Voice Search

Conversational searches are used more on mobile devices. Why is that? In a pure logic way of thinking this makes no sense as conversational searches are in most cases longer search queries. That does not fit well with the fast world of mobile, does it? Add to that that typing search queries on mobile devices still is a challenge for people who are not born with a mobile in one of their hands (such as myself). But logic is the wrong approach here. The answer cannot be found with our left brains when it is a right brain behavior. Smartphones are becoming more and more our personal friends, maybe even our BFF (Best Friends Forever for those who don't have daughters on elementary schools). Writing these words I just came back from an online marketing exposition in London where they offered many info sessions. I noticed that when a person took the seat next to another person no words were exchanged, not even a smile was offered. I am sure they were very friendly and fine people but they were all engulfed into their smartphones, even during sessions. I must admit that I myself copied this behavior otherwise I was the only one sitting as a lame duck.

Voice Search will boost our conversational searches even more. Now we can talk to our greatest of friends and what's more, it answers back in a fine and intelligent voice.

How do conversational searches differ?

Conversational search queries may lead to the same search engine results than utilitarian searches. Maybe for now, but that will change. Remember, our audience is using the emotional right brain by applying a conversational search query. The perfect match should be a webpage that taps into this right brain search. How to do it? First we have to acknowledge the difference between conversational searches and utilitarian searches.

These are the main issues we will have to consider:

1. Much longer search queries

Instead of combining one or two keywords people use whole sentences including these keywords. This makes it more difficult for search engines to discern the important keywords from the non-relevant keywords. Take this query for example: "Which anti dandruff shampoo to buy when travelling to India?". In this sentence two different search themes are included, shampoo and travel to India. Still Google knows what we are looking for (some years ago they didn't). In fact I tried different combinations and in most cases Google and Bing got it right. That's great of course, especially considering that it is up to us to make the perfect match.

2. Question oriented search queries

Most conversational searches are in the form of a question. That offers some challenges to search engines as most website content offers answers. In many cases however the answer is not found in the question. That makes perfect sense again, otherwise we didn't have to ask it in the first place. Matching questions and answers is the real challenge for search engines in conversational searches.

3. Search queries aimed at personal advice

Most conversational searches are looking for a tailor made answer that perfectly suits the person who made the query. This is another challenge for both search engines and website content managers. How in earth can we be relevant to each individual?

Best practices for SEO in conversational searches

So how can we tap into this conversational search shift? What can we do differently to drive conversational searches to our website?

These tips will help:

A) Write explanatory copy

Conversational searches try to get deeper and more specific answers. In explaining your products and services you may create the perfect match to a conversational search query. "Can I use my smartphone aboard a United Airlines flight?" will match your webpage content in which you describe the use of smartphones during UA flights. Never forget: there is much more to be explained about the proposition you offer than you would think. Try to explain your product from all sorts of angles.

B) Write conversational copy

Personal questions are best met with personal answers. This works twofold. First, in writing in a conversational manner you will use the same kind of words and combinations that will make up questions. We already saw the use of words like "can" "should" and "need" in searches. When you write in a conversational manner you will almost automatically use these words too. That will increase the likelihood that your copy will match the query better than that of non-conversational copy. Second, when someone uses a right brain conversational query your conversational copy will perfectly match this persons expectations. This will have a positive impact on conversions.

C) Use questions within your copy

Why not using the same questions your target audience could be using? It will give you an extra angle form which to approach your proposition. Try to ask yourself questions about your products and services and there will be a reasonable chance that you will come up with the same questions as your target audience. Answering these questions will provide great website content and a perfect match with some conversational searches.

D) Write in a person-to-person style

In general this is sound advice in content creation. Never forget: you are not speaking to your target audience, there isn't an audience at all. You are speaking to just one person. So, however open your website content is, how many "traffic" your pages will get, your articles will be read by 1 person at a time. So why not be personal or even intimate. Imagine yourself talking to a new friend, just the two of you, alone on a quiet sunny afternoon, sitting on a couch, overlooking the busy streets form a rooftop apartment, drinking your favorite drink, nibbling some salted peanuts. No one will hear you, no one will see you sitting there. Feel free to talk, conversate, get into each other's brains. You get the picture?

So, what to do?

- Before writing an article think of your Tone of Voice, you might want to switch to a more conversational one.
- Try being helpful, share advice, you are an intimate friend for the time they read your article.

Most important

Think of that 1 person you are writing for. You may use a persona. Talk, don't speak!

9] Show the downside

Total average SEO impact: ★★★★

In essence SEO is supplying answers to what people want to know. They are using a search engine because they are searching, that makes sense. But what are they searching for? If they are in a buying mood (and we marketeers love people who are in that particular state of mind) they want to know all the ins and outs of the product they are interesting in. That makes sense too. They want to know how this product or service will solve their problems. But they also want to know if there are some downsides to consider. Will the product always work in any circumstance? What if it breaks down? May it break down? Is this really what solves the problem? Of course you and I can add some more questions about the negative side of buying a product or service. Especially with high end expensive products we want to know what the other side of the moon looks like. Will we get that answer? Not from most suppliers that are selling the product.

So what do we all do, we will search again with words like "disadvantages" or "why not buy" or "downsides" or even more dismal "do not buy [name of brand]". Where will our search query land? Right, on the far side of the moon. On some consumer forum where negativity rules the waves. Mind, there are a number of good forums out there but if you really search for the negative, you will get what you are looking for, big time.

Do we as online marketing beings want this to happen? I don't think so. We are talking about potential buyers who are on the brink of ordering. They were on our website and we sent them into dark space where they encountered unknown anonymous mooncrawlers with an attitude (it must be hard of course, living in the cold and dark looking at our blue planet day in and day out).

Cheerleaders are great, but they are useless in scoring points

We cannot expect our audiences to take us serious when all we do is praising ourselves. People know that there are downsides. You know them too. Just tell them. That hurts doesn't it, writing about some negative factors of your great product and service? I know, it's like going to your weekly AA meeting, honesty is difficult. Self-reflection is hard.
The truth however is that people actively are searching for the downside. Just type in your favorite brand + the word "negative". Well, don't do it when you want to keep it your favorite brand. With large global brands you will get on average more than 30 million hits. Active negative searches like brandname + disadvantages will get you more or less the same amount of hits. Maybe you might think that we are talking about just a small portion of the internet users who thrive on negativity. Forget it! That is not the case. People just want to know what they are spending their money on. Don't blame them for doing their homework. We as marketing professionals just ignore our target audience's craving for information. As this book is about SEO and not particularly about conversion optimization (although they are intertwined) there are obvious gains to make when you do address the downside of your product. Your target audience is actively searching for it, so give it to them. Besides, your competitor is just as cowardly as you are, so you can really score some organic volume here.

How to handle it?

There is a challenge of course. Talking negatively about your own product or service will not be easy and will probably be met by some raised eyebrows within your organization. Not a simple task. But there are ways to manage it. Let us discuss some suggestions:

1. Let other people raise the downside

Reviews are great in mixing the positive with the negative. So please use them wherever it is possible. What they do not do properly however, is attracting negative searches. That is because the review content is often on an outside platform (the website of the review provider). So looking at it from a direct SEO impact it will not bring you much extra traffic. But, indirectly, you will not lose traffic if you can show the negative through your reviews. People are less tempted to abandon your site and type in an extra negative search term in Google or Bing. That is a win. Another option is to showcase the reviews directly on your site, that will help you in attracting some negative searches.

2. Address the disadvantages in an open way

When you are a great copy writer you know that words make the difference and there is so much you can do to add some nuance to your sentences. Remember, the writer is always in control. There are many ways to address the downside without being destructive. Suppose you are a carmaker, why not compare your product with that of your competitors just being honest. If that other car is more spacious it doesn't hurt to tell that. Your car is maybe more economic because of that. When making comparisons and your product beats that of your competitor's on all points it is just not trustworthy anymore. If you think your customers are fools, it is you who is crazy. There is no harm done if you list up the positives and negatives in an open way. If you are a lawyer and you are more expensive than others why not tell it. You should be better then, just explain that you are and show that your win-rate is higher (if it's not, stop overcharging please). If you sell running shoes you can tell your public that they have a superb shock absorption for the first 500 miles, after that they will underperform. That is honesty people dig. Just write about it, create specific pages addressing advantages and disadvantages. They are great in attracting traffic, besides it will add to your trustworthiness, and that will not tear down your brand, it will lift it up.

3. Write about issues of the past

Former bankruptcies, issues with safety that were in the news, really negative things. What to do with them? Put them on specific pages. They do not have to be within the menu. There may be some active search still going on about issues with a huge impact of the past. What do you want? Let other people tell your story or do you think you can explain it better and more balanced? I think you will have to opt for the latter. That doesn't mean you have to advertise them on your site, but when someone is searching for it, do your best in directing this search to your webpage. This isn't hard to do in general as a search for your brand name + negative story will stand a good chance in getting a high ranking on this query.

So, what to do?

- Addres the negative, no harm in telling the truth.
- Balance the negative with the positive, every downside has an upside, no need to hold it back.

Most important

Do not underestimate your audience, if they can't find it here they will find it anywhere.

10] What's in it For Me?

Total average SEO impact: ★★★

The impact of "for me" searches

Search queries with the addition "for me" are growing exponentially. According to Google, searches with "for me" in it grow with 30% annually. People aren't looking for general answers when searching, they want specific answers, tailored to their needs. But what do people expect to get when typing in something like "best personal loan for me" or "which car type is right for me"? I think they ultimately want to really receive precisely the answer to that question. Just one hit with: "This is it!". That is maybe why the most "for me" searches are typed into smartphones, the most intimate digital friend one keeps. Of course, that is not what is happening for now. But with the advent of Voice Search and using the data you leave behind while surfing the net it won't be for long that you will get that perfect answer back from your search engines. In fact, I think they already can deliver that but that is not always in the interest of search engines with an advertising model in place. But this too can be solved.

How to tap into "for me" searches

Looking at the results search engines come up with when typing a "for me" search query you will see that these types of websites gain the most of them:

1. **Websites with filter tools**
   Think of car sales platforms where you can find

used cars by brands and a number of other filters.

2. **Comparison sites**
   Comparing one energy supplier with another is an
   example of a result that may come up when typing
   "best energy supplier for me".

3. **Conversational webpages**
   A "for me" query is a personal query by definition.
   Meeting this query with a conversational answer
   makes sense. Talking about "you and me" and
   giving tips and advice in a conversational manner
   may be the perfect match for the searcher and the
   engines that do the matching.

Some extra tips

- **Use the interview model**
  Questions and answers are ideally suited to get on
  the "me and you" level. Besides that, they really are
  a joy to read instead of some dreary summing up of
  features and benefits. Let some customers and
  stakeholders share their thoughts. What do they
  think about your company, products and services?
  "Well, for me, it was the best decision to start
  working here".
  "I really love this new design"
  "For me personally, I would have done without the
  strawberries, but the cake is awesome"

- **Name product and usage**
  In many "for me" searches you will find search
  terms like product and usages. Think of searches
  like "the best razor blades for trimming beards for

me" or "best ergonomic office chair for me". These queries try to guide the search engine in doing its work but ultimately they have a great confidence in their search engine's understanding of what they really need.

- **Sum up features, specifications and benefits**
  This is more a conversion tip although it also helps in driving organic "for me" traffic. People who type a "for me" search into a search bar are looking for a personal answer to their quest. When they land on your page they want to be convinced that this is precisely what they were looking for. So you need to persuade people with features and benefits. Think of the golden rule of "What's in it for me?" (meaning what's in it for that other "me" that may become your customer). Never forget: We are all "me's". Every "you" is a "me"!

So, what to do?

- Think of what people want when typing in a "for me" search query.
- Address features and benefits that are of particular interest of certain target audiences.
- Use a conversational Tone of Voice and view your proposition from a "for me" angle.

Most important

What people really want is a product or service tailored to their specific needs. Get into that, make sure that you address the benefits on a personal level.

11] You're so close to me

Total average SEO impact: ★★★

Tapping into "near me" searches

Searches with the phrase "near me" added are becoming extremely popular. According to Google we see a 500% increase in "near me" searches during the last couple of years. Of course, the bulk of this traffic comes from mobile searches, but not all. When you are logged into your laptop at home these searches also make sense.
Initially a "near me" search is intended to find products or services near the place I am right now, sounds logic doesn't it. But there is more to it. Today we also expect an instant solution. It is a very active kind of search query. We are willing to act upon it. When I search for a "gas station near me" I probably am sweating it out hoping to make it to the next station where I can fill it up. If I search for "pizza near me" I am probably very hungry and decided what I want to eat, right now!

We also see more specific queries with "near me" added but without the urgency, one would think. A search query like "Levi's pants for sale near me" is just a way of telling my search engine that I am into buying a Levi's, I just want to know where (and the following question may be one for Google Maps, giving me directions how to find it). What's important about "near me" searches is its active character. These are people on the brink of becoming a customer. Question is, will they find you?

How to get on the radar with "near me" searches?

There are several ways you may prepare your website content to receive these hot searches.

1. Make sure your address is on your webpage

"Near me" searches are always local searches. One way to attract them is relying on the tracking techniques of smartphones, wifi's and log-ins on your desktops (such as a Google account log-in). Your address and your Google My Business webpage play important roles here. My advice is always to put your address on each and every webpage instead of only putting it on your contact page. This helps combining search queries with locations. If one of your webpage is the perfect match for the search query without the "near me", your address on that page may make it also the perfect match for the "near me" phrase included.

2. Write on a local search level

What I mean is that if you are a shop or business that serves a local audience propagate that fact. Go into your local authority, your perfect service in a named area, describe your local history and bond with local initiatives. The more local you appear the more local search engines will view you.

3. Give full information and prices!

Remember, this is an active group. They want to shop. So give them all the information they need to say "Yes, that's what I'm looking for"! So, please name prices of your products. Give full details. Do not waste their precious time!

So, what to do?

- Think local, make sure your website is optimized for local search, add your address, make the local connection.

Most important

Showcase your physical address, add information about parking possibilities, add opening hours, these people want to come by in person.

12] Tell me a long story

Total average SEO impact: ★★★★★

The long-form copy debate

There is much debate going on about the length of your webpage copy. Good communication should be short, clear and to-the-point. We have all learned that in high school. This is the moment to forget about that, well... only the first part. It still has to be clear and to-the-point. That's a challenge of course, writing lengthy copy about a topic that is still relevant. But there is more to it than just long-form copy. It is not always true to begin with. Sometimes short specific copy will win the SEO battle over longer copy. This is especially the case with answering very specific questions or providing definitions. In general long copy wins however. I will explain why and, more importantly, how to write long, relevant and even specific copy about a topic without boring your audience to death and without falling asleep yourself.

The impact of long-form copy

Why does long copy beat short copy in SEO? These are the main reasons:

1. Search engines prefer complete answers (as your questions are a bit vague)

Many search queries are questions even if they do not come with a question mark. You want to know or find something when you are searching for something. Problem is that in most cases your question is a bit broad. It lacks specifics. When you type "organic search results" what are you looking for? Probably you want to learn more insights about organic search results. But what kind of insights is not clear. What should Google do? If I were Google I would offer you search results that offer as much relevant insights about organic search results if possible. That is precisely what Google offers you. In most cases this implies long copy.

2. Search engines love depth and opinions

Search engines are not robots (well in fact they are, but let's be quiet about that, they hate that name). They know the difference between good copy and bad. They know when you went to your limits in tackling a topic, viewing it from all angles, supplying a balanced opinion. If someone is searching why not supply them with high-quality content? A webpage where you will be submerged in answers and opinions about exactly the topic you are interested in. Search engines are nice and understanding, they know what you want to read. So they give it to you (for free!). In-depth copy, shining a light on a topic from all angles, naming advantages and disadvantages, supplying some practical tips, it will all add to the supreme quality of your content. And let's face it, you can't do that in 300 words.

3. It's a matter of math

Don't underestimate this one. Roughly 70% of all search queries fall into the Long Tail category. How to find the perfect match for Long Tails is a quest for search engines. In most cases a Long Tail consists of a combination of 2 or 3 different search themes that in most cases are related. In other cases there is no relationship whatsoever, on first sight. Let's explore these different Long Tails queries. This is a Long Tail with a relationship between themes: "fall protection for working on atriums in high rise buildings". Here the themes "fall protection", "atriums" and "high rise buildings" are combined in 1 single search query. What would be a great match for this query? Of course a webpage that is talking about using fall protection working on atriums in high rise buildings. This is an in-depth search query that asks for a webpage that is touching these themes. There are not many webpages that match this query exactly, although it is not a strange query. There is logic in it. That being said, it is not covered in a specific webpage. But when you are writing a substantial webpage about the challenges of using fall protection in high rises you may coincidentally write about the use of atriums in high rise buildings. The longer your copy the likelier the possibility is that you touch on some logic combinations.

What about non-related Long Tails? Consider this query: "hiring a car in New York coming by train from Philadelphia". Sounds logic too but here some non-related themes are combined. "train" and "car", "New York" and "Philadelphia". Making it worse is the confusion between arrivals (New York) and departures (Philadelphia). When you use this phrase in Google you will learn that search results will come up with webpages that offer car hires in New York and in Philadelphia. The train station is ignored in most cases. Suppose you had written a webpage about inbound trains from Philadelphia and the nearest car rentals in the area of the most common NY train station it most certainly would have come up. These are all **accidental matches** that emanate from long copy webpages. You do not intend to match for these specific long tail queries but in writing long-form copy your chances of hitting the perfect match increase drastically.

So how to write long-form copy?

First you will have to think about the search theme you are trying to tackle. Is it a highly competitive theme? Then long copy makes sense. Is it a broad theme with many related subthemes? Then long copy will definitely be the answer.

But where to begin and how to start?

My advice:

1. Begin with defining your theme

Tell about what you are going to write and explain in general terms what your theme is all about.

2. Explore your theme

Supply characteristics, give examples, write about traits and specifications.

3. View your topic from all angles

Are there any downsides or conflicting thoughts? Show them.

4. Talk about usability and practical issues

Combine your theme with other subthemes. Delve into practical uses and showcase solutions in different situations.

5. Supply tips and advice

Try helping your audience on their path to purchase or help them in their considerations. Whenever you are approaching a writer's block a practical tip will keep you writing.

What's the problem with long-form copy?

There is only one problem: It will take time and tap all your energy. I have only one thing to say to that: A well-written long-form copy will bring you lots of organic traffic for many, many years to come. The blood, sweat and tears of today will be paid back with dividends for as long as 5 to 10 years and even beyond that.

How long should my copy be?

Forget that question. When you tackle all ins and outs about a search theme you know when you are ready. That's the time to quit. For lovers of figures. Think in the range of 1.500 to 2.500 words.

Choosing your theme

There is one issue I have to add to this discussion. When choosing your search time, pick one that is specific. It's no use to write a long-form copy about "shoes". It is in the specific themes that long copy will make the difference. Writing about "measuring the size of your feet" is a perfect one. Another would be: "choosing the right shoe laces". Of course it depends on your market but too general themes are not suited. Too specific makes your work hard of course, but that is precisely why you can make the difference.

So, what to do?

- Take your time for writing a content page, you are in it for the long term.
- Take the helicopter view when writing, make sure to describe things from all angles.
- Name advantages, disadvantages, practical examples, projects, just be thorough.
- When your inspiration is empty try personal tips.

Most important

1 hour spent more now on writing content may mean the difference between 0 and 1.000 visitors to that page, you do not waste energy in writing long-form copy, you will waste it when writing too short copy.

13] EAT that!

Total average SEO impact: ★★★★★

It's all about Expertise, Authoritativeness & Trustworthiness

Looking at your webpage from a search engine's perspective it is this what they are looking for. If your webpage shows Expertise, Authoritativeness and Trustworthiness (EAT) your search engine will treat your webpage with respect and gives you the best and first seat in the waiting room we call the search engine result page. I do not make this up, Google explicitly acknowledges that EAT is one of the most important ranking factors. That leaves us with the question: How to become a trusted expert with authority? Hmm, that sounds like a bit of work. It does.

What is expertise?

Pure knowledge, not only in theory but also in practice. You are not an expert when you just graduated as a heart surgeon. You must understand your line of business, be able to distinguish the rubbish from the gems, see through the mist others create. It doesn't come overnight, it takes time to absorb the facts and give them the meaning they deserve. Also important: you cannot become an expert in all fields, it requires specialization. Are you an expert? Do you know your trade? How long can you teach others about your business? Are you done in an hour or can you talk about your profession from dawn till dusk?

How to let Google know you're an expert?

I know some truly great experts. My father is one of them. He was an expert in production process optimizations, customers who got to know his expertise never wanted another. If you would ask me to name an expert in web design I could give you a few names. Problem is, Google doesn't know. In the case of my father he is forgiven, he already excelled in his job before the dawn of the internet. But if you are an expert in your field and you can use some extra business just being great doesn't suffice, you must prove it to the Googles of the world. How? The answer is simple, share your knowledge. Write about your business, give away all the ins and outs you know, supply advice, share tips. Just let it all out!

But if I do that, who wants to pay for my expertise?

If selling your expertise is what makes you earn your daily bread it makes no sense to give it all away for free. Does it? Yes, it does! It makes perfect sense to disperse your knowhow, 100% free as if you were Santa Claus. Just giving, no taking. Why? 3 reasons:

1. It's the only way to let others know you know your trade

You may claim to be an expert, you might let others tell that you are but only by showing your expertise will people see for themselves that you deserve this title. For new customers who do not know your name you must proof that you are worth their time and money. There are not many souls out there that fall for the line "I'm the best that's ever been". Your website content must breathe expertise. It should give away exactly what they are searching for. People will respond by: "thanks for the information, this guy or girl knows what he /she is talking about". Will they pick up the phone and tell you to come over right now? No, they won't, not for now, maybe never. But that's not a problem, somewhere, in the back of one's head, a few brain cells will store this information and add to it: "I was touched by an expert".

2. It's the only way to let search engines know there is an expert "in da house"

Search engines do not take things for granted. Claims of expertise don't mean sh#t to them. They want to see and hear your expertise by your website content. What they are looking for is the perfect match for a search query and they know that giving silly answers to smart questions will not bring them praise and glory. What does a search engine do, 24 hours of every single day? They go through an amazing amount of website content. They crawl through heaps of content and most of it is pure senseless rubbish, the same stuff all over again and again. And once in a while they too are touched by this great article, this jewel of a webpage that just plainly explains in all color and finesse the answers to WHAT, HOW and WHY. They too will remember this when it will be convenient, when the time is right, when someone searches for the answers you supplied.

3. Don't let Do-It-Yourselfers bother you

What would have become of our human race without this special breed of man? We don't know who invented the wheel but I'll bet it was a Do-It-Yourselfer. A stubborn, fool hearted, headstrong go-getter who ignores the help of others and want to solve a problem all by him- or herself. The world's greatest inventions as well as its biggest failures have been accomplished by Do-It-Yourselfers. What do they do? They suck in all the information that is available, they want to learn all the tricks of the trade and then apply them on their own. That is not selfish behavior. It isn't piggyback riding. They just want to do things by themselves. Nothing wrong with that, even respectable. I tell you this because this is what you are afraid of. That someone is "stealing" your expertise and apply it by him- or herself without paying you for it. Let me tell you one thing about Do-It-Yourselfers: They are what they are, they would never have become a customer of yours, they are not part of your target audience. You will never lose business to a Do-It-Yourselfer. There is no downside. There even is an upside. They go through your pages, they have the longest Time on Sites of all visitors (because they are the only ones that really read all your stuff) and indirectly they propel your webpages to the best spots of search engine result pages. Hail to the Do-It-Yourselfer!

From Expertise to Authority

Becoming an expert isn't easy. Becoming an authority in your field is even beyond that. What's the difference between an expert and an authority? You can work to become an expert, it's all up to you. Not so with authority. It's a prize you may get when you excel in expertise and other people recognize you as THE source of know-it-all. Is there nothing you can do about it? Well there is plenty to do, but the final verdict of authoritativeness is in the eye of the beholder. What can you do? Share your expertise by all sorts of media and stages. Speak about your expertise, write about it, help people with it. Spread the word!

How Google assesses authoritativeness

Google is on the look-out for authoritativeness. It's the excellence of expertise they crave for. As a search engine they look at authority through the lens of website content. They want to show the best website content on a search query coming from a respectable source. A source with authority. It is not only what is being said but who is saying it that counts. But how does that work? First and foremost search engines want to know who is responsible for the webpage content. Think of Contact pages with a full address included, About Us pages with lengthy information about the background of who's behind the website and supplying information about the writer of a single webpage or blogpost. That is the first part of assessing authority. Then it depends on the authority of this person or organization that is behind the webpage content. Search engines have a myriad of ways to establish authority. Let's name a few:

1. Backlinks form other respectable sources that lead to a webpage or website

2. Search volume on the name of the writer of webpage content
3. Branded search volume on the name of the organization or website
4. Number of places that a particular name of person or brand will pop up in other websites or social media
5. Returning visitors that come back to more website content of the same website
6. Number of shares of webpage

Becoming an authority in your field takes time and efforts. It also depends on your line of business. When you are active in the health industry the webpage content written by a well-known physician will be more authoritative than that written by an active health blogger. But if this blogger has established a large following of active readers he or she may outperform the physician, even on authoritativeness.

Can I trust you?

This is a question that is at the essence of human interaction. Are you telling the truth? Don't you have ulterior motives? Are you someone I can depend upon? You may be viewed as an expert, you may be an authority in your field but this all means nothing if you cannot be trusted. Trust is the most important trait in a human being, it connects the inner soul with the outer behavior. You might wonder if an expert with authority may exist without trust? Well, that depends. There are many cases that expertise, authority and trust prevail until that final moment of truth when everything collapses. Think of the Bernie Madoffs of this world who run Ponzi schemes to lure investors money. They use their "expertise" and authority to gain access to people's money. Trust builds up as high returns are made possible by still higher deposits of customers and when this flywheel of fortune dries up the whole house of cards implodes. The same may be true about some world leaders that use trust the other way around. They are trusted with people's votes based upon alleged expertise of running the country and when they are in power they build authority to hold control. Trust is given by someone else, you may use it to reinforce it or misuse it to mislead the giver.

How to establish trust on webpages?

First, make sure that what you're saying is right. That is not the same as saying that you cannot express your own meaning or give your own interpretation of something. On the contrary! But do not say things that are completely rubbish. Not so long ago I was attending an event where a person gave a presentation about the use of social media. This guy was a so-called expert on its subject, he was an authority (he wrote about 10 books) but a couple of things he was telling were absolutely nonsense. They were so besides the truth that for me he lost all his credibility. If these couple of things were so outright false what should I think about all the other non verifiable things he was telling me? He lost his trustworthiness right at that point. I must add that trustworthiness is a personal thing. You may gain it or lose it one person at a time. After the presentation other people told me: "Hey, that guy was really great, didn't you think so?". I was lost in frustration…

Besides telling the truth, trustworthiness comes forth from being authentic. Share your views, explain complicated matters, but always do it in your own authentic voice. That will build credibility and trustworthiness. Think of your Tone of Voice, writing webpages in your own style will adhere to a specific audience. It will establish a match with a like minded person (and may also repel not like minded persons). Will search engines pick up your trustworthiness? They do if what you are saying makes sense. It also helps if you publish more of the same high quality web content. They may see you as a source for good reliable content on a specific theme.
Another powerful way to build up trust for search engines is sharing original and authentic news on a regular basis. A daily blog about your specific market will in time generate expertise, authoritativeness and trustworthiness. As long as you can come up with really original and authentic content that is right on the spot!

So, what to do?

- Showcase your expertise.
- Write in an authentic way using a consistent Tone of Voice.
- Verify claims and figures, be sure to tell the truth.
- Concentrate on your website but writing on other platforms will help .
- Write a book about your expertise (it's fun!).
- Add new content expressing your expertise on a regular basis.
- Make it possible to get back to you, use newsletters and email subscriptions.

Most important

Give away all you know. They will pay you for expertise in action.

14] Slow, slow, quick

Total average SEO impact: ★★★

Slow searches for fast deals

For people who are born with a bargain DNA, retailers have invented deal days. We all know them and most of us have been swayed by them. Black Friday, Cyber Monday, Amazon Prime Day, Tax-free weekends, Single's Day, we marketeers have invented all sorts of names to lure shoppers with great once-in-a-lifetime deals. What's the deal of the deal-day? You will get the deal if you decide and buy right now. So the exchange that is taking place is low price for speed. There is no room for thinking it over, it is right here, right now. Right? Wrong!

Don't underestimate the deal shopper

Research from Google shows that 60% of deal seekers research before they buy on deal-day. In fact a large part of this group is actively searching for products for months prior to some deal-days (especially Black Friday). They compare product details and shop way before D-Day is at hand. What does that mean? Well, first of all, your sales of deal-day do not fall form the sky. You probably had the honor to receive this customer many, many times before during the last months. Second, you are not the lurer of your customer, it is you who is being lured. If your deal price is disappointing you bet that your potential customer clicks to that other shop he or she has listed. Lowest price wins, no emotion, no guilt, bye, bye. No buy.

Is this bad or good for business?

I don't know. Depends on you. If you are in a position to make the best deal in the market and make a profit then deal days are great. In fact, if you grasp the habits and mindset of the professional emotionless deal seeker you can optimize your sales even more. If however you cannot meet the demands of this peculiar group of deal seekers, this 60% of professional, ruthless, how-low-can-you-go shophoppers, you may have to alter your strategy. Then go for this 40% of deal buyers, the ones that are familiar with your shop, the loyal customers that also love a deal but do not make it an Eldoradian quest.

But how does this all impact your SEO strategy?

There are several impacts here. First, you will receive organic traffic during the year that is deal-oriented. It is coming from people with that bargain DNA in them, they can't help it and you can't cure them. So what do you do? You cozy up to them. You will give them what they are after. Make deals throughout the year and put them on a specific page. That will boost your conversions but may hurt your profits (depends of course). There are several options you can pursue. You may hide this Outlet page from your menu to shield this page from your regular visitors or you may be all open on this. More importantly, you will SEO this Outlet page on terms like Outlet, Sales, Discounts, Bargains, Deals, you get the drift. By doing that you will make this particular page more relevant on these search terms. That is a plus as these deal buyers do use these terms in their search terms. They can't resist using them although they know it is not Deal Day yet. Moreover, some can't resist a deal when they see one. Maybe they will not wait until Deal Day comes along, remember these are people too who sometimes have their moments of weakness and want to have it right here, right now!

Second, not all your organic or paid search traffic is ready to buy right now. That is not news but part of this audience is specifically gathering information to use on deal days. What do they look for? Specifications, product reviews and prices of course. They are making their shortlists. Will you be on them? Make sure to give them all they need to know to make comparisons. They want to know that you offer the precise product they are looking for. So go through your product pages. This group of customers is very much into product details so instead of optimizing your category pages (which makes perfect sense as they will match high volume search terms consisting of general product names such as "running shoes") you also must optimize your product pages. These deal seekers know what they want. They go for terms like "Nike Air Zoom Pegasus 35 Shield iD" So make sure your product and brand names are in order and give them all the details they want (no duplicate content please!).

Third, deal seekers love comparing offers. In fact, that is the addiction they thrive on. Always looking for still lower prices, never contented with the offer at hand. This urge for searching and comparing leads to many clicks. They don't bother to come back at your site again and again and as they are relentless in getting what they want, they see no harm in clicking a zillion times on your Google or Bing Ads. That may be a problem for you. Do not underestimate it, I have seen numerous conversion paths that included more than 20 clicks on Google Ads. These paths eventually did convert (not to mention the ones that didn't). But at what cost? Go to your Analytics account and go through your conversion path metrics, what does it tell you? If you are active in a B2C market I bet you will see the same. These are not all deal seekers for Deal Day but they are in the same "shopping" mood. What to do about it? If the problem is severe you may cancel your ads for specific branded products, because that is were the biggest problems arise. Sometimes it is better to advertise on a level higher in the sales funnel, the more generic themes and product category searches. To counter balance this you must focus on SEO for your branded product pages. So one strategy is putting more effort on SEO on your product detail pages and switching your Google and Bing search ads from branded product search to product category search.

To give an example: Say you are in the running shoes market. Instead of using search ads on terms like "Nike Air Zoom Pegasus 35 Shield iD" you go for "Nike running shoes" with your Google and Bing search ads. Instead of SEO-ing solely on "Nike running shoes" (which again makes perfect sense) you put all efforts in optimizing your product detail pages like "Nike Air Zoom Pegasus 35 Shield iD". I know, this all goes right into the existing logic of SEO and search ads. But doing something completely different sometimes makes sense (not in a Monty Python way of course).

So, what to do?

- Deal seekers are primarily comparative buyers. Offer them all product details, reviews and buying information.
- Deal seekers are brand-shoppers. They want the best brands at the lowest prices. Ask yourself the question that you are able to offer exactly that. If your margins are too low you may decide to forget about this target group.
- Make a strategic decision about SEO efforts and search ads. Go through your Analytics and look at conversion paths. Giving away a big chunk of your retail margin to make the perfect deal is painful enough. Do not underestimate the additional cost of high volume clicks coming from this group months before Deal Day has come to town.

Most important

Focus your attention on the product detail pages. This is where deal seekers want to learn all about product and prices.

15] Bye bye backlinks

Total average SEO impact: ★★★

Don't bother about backlinks

Some 10 to 15 years ago the Holy Grail of our nascent SEO science evolved around backlinks. The idea was that getting the right backlinks would automatically boost your organic traffic. Did it ever work? Nah, not really but that was not the point. If you could get some truly great backlinks from authoritative websites it was time to party. All the results that were coming in months after this great victorious day were of course directly related to getting these backlinks. I will tell you know to forget about backlinks. Theoretically they may still work but in practice it is all a waste of time. If you do not believe in fairy tales you must not believe in backlinks.

How did backlinks became so important?

I think it was around 2003 or 2004 that PageRank and backlinks became the focus of newly established SEO agencies. In these early years of Google's advent as number 1 search engine there was much discussion going on about ranking factors. Google officials were often asked about its algorithms and some of them answered that getting links from other authoritative websites was the most important ranking factor. So how did we as SEO agencies respond to that? In a Pavlovian way: "Well, if you want backlinks, we will supply them, by the zillions". But of course that was not what Google meant about the importance of backlinks.

What was (and still is) the SEO power of backlinks?

I just told you to forget about backlinks. To twist your mind, here I will state the opposite (I love doing that). Seen from Google's perspective an original truly authentic backlink works like this:

Website A is a great website that offers a bunch of high quality information about some topic, let's say it is about starting your own business (for all Millennials who do not know what that means, it's the same thing as having a Startup but with less money to burn and more sweat to evaporate). This website covers all sorts of practical tips and pitfalls to evade when starting on your own. It also has a page about tax implications and tax plans for starters but on this page it will only scratch the surface of this subject. Here they show a link to the most relevant pages of the IRS (the American Tax Authority). By doing that website A admits that they lack all the information you can find on the IRS website. Website A is telling their audience: "you really should read this stuff you will find on that website, it is better and more thorough than mine". Website B (the IRS website) obtains a backlink from website A and search engines like Google who regard website A as authoritative on starting your own business will learn that concerning tax implications for starters the IRS website is even more authoritative (well, if more backlinks like that will appear on other similar websites). In essence a forward link (the link placed on website A) is a vote for relevance for website B. So the backlink received by website B builds on authority and relevance based upon the website (the authority of the whole website) and the page (the relevant content). Sounds great does it? So it works fine, getting these backlinks? Yes, if these conditions are met:

1. Website A is an authoritative website
2. The webpage where the forward link is on is relevant to the webpage that receives this link (the backlink)
3. The link is a "do-follow" link that transmits link juice to the receiving website B

There is no such thing as a free lunch

A backlink that works must have all these 3 characteristics. So this backlink must be a "do-follow" link coming from an authoritative website within your market. By the way, a do-follow link will transmit link juice and subsequently the giver will lose juice by giving it away (it's a win-lose game). That may be no problem in our example but in most cases it is. No-follow links only pass traffic but no juice so it does not boost your SEO power directly (it may be doing it a bit indirectly but that is besides the idea of backlinks as SEO boosters). As an active linkbuilder you may try to persuade authoritative websites to give you a link. If you like frustrations this will be your dream job. Why on earth should an authoritative website link to your website so you can grow your business? You have great website content? Maybe, but I will tell you that online authorities do not give a heck about your website. And if you will finally score a link, why would they make a do-follow link? What you will get on a very sunny day will be a no-follow link coming from a website with no authority at all. In supplying a do-follow link website A will lose authority on that specific theme and in most cases they do not want to lose a thing, especially not to a low authority website like yours. Okay, so you also are an authority in your field, that may change things, but still getting a do-follow link will be extremely hard.

So we must forget about backlinks?

No, we must go back to the original intention of Google's statement that backlinks are an important ranking factor. What they meant is that by organic growth of your website you may assemble backlinks coming from other websites that will link to your website content. If a particular page will be of interest of a third party and they will link to that it is a plus. It happens if (and only if) your webpage content is really great and touches on a specific issue. Of course it also depends on the organization behind this website. The IRS and other public services will gather more backlinks than an online shop for pet food. Major brands like Apple, Nike and Ferrari will automatically get backlinks when new models and products are coming to the market.

It is your content, stupid!

Why did I write this chapter in this book? It may be a bit confusing. I tell you to forget about backlinks (and I mean that) and simultaneously I tell you that backlinks still are a ranking factor. What I try to convey is the following: Do not put your time and energy in getting backlinks from other websites. Put all your energy in your website content. Backlinks may come automatically and if they don't (which is pretty realistic for the bulk of websites out there) your website content will drive organic traffic thanks to search engines that will match your great content with all relevant search queries consisting of keyword combinations and Long Tails.

So, what to do?

- Focus all your attention in writing great website content.
- Make sharing easy.

- The more specific your article or page the more likely you will get a backlink.
- Stop wasting your time scoring inferior no-follow backlinks.
- Enjoy life! Stop begging for backlinks. Get your ass behind a desk and write!

Most important

SEO is a very time consuming effort. That is its greatest asset too. Shortcuts do not work (anymore). Bye, bye fast guys and gals, hello diligent workers! Your sweat in writing great content will outdo all these easy-thinking backlink builders. Isn't that great!

16] Goodbye sales funnel, Hello search

Total average SEO impact: ★★★★★

Sales funnels are history

In fact, they never existed. Now we have the data to support it. Sales funnels are like astronauts walking on the moon. If you tell a story over and over again, if you have people of high regard explaining in detail how it all works, showing images that make sense, people will believe you. Wait a minute, am I saying here that I don't believe we went to the moon and back? Eh, let's forget about that before you think I am a total nutcase (but no, I don't believe it, yes, you may laugh). Let's get back at sales funnels. We used to learn that people buy products and services in a linear way. How does it work? We have a need to fulfill, we will search in broader terms for solutions to our problem, some brands and products do appeal to us, we dig in a little deeper and we buy. Sounds logic, must be right. It isn't.
Research from Google shows that people search in a non-linear illogic way sometimes narrowing, sometimes broadening their span of attention. Ultimately they will find the product or service they were looking for but the path to this final conversion is winding and often incomprehensible. It is like booking a family holiday with your mother-in-law. All options will be discussed, wild explorations will be put on the table but at the end you will find yourself in the same hotel on the same beach as each and every year (I want to stress that this is a pure fictional remark…).

To give an example. Let's say you want to buy a new car. By searching online you may start with your favorite brand. If that would be a Mercedes you will type in something like "Mercedes models". You will go through the site and you will go to the model you like, maybe a Mercedes C-class. The next search may be "Mercedes C used car" as you might think that a new one is rather expensive. You may visit some used cars platforms and the next linear and logic step would be that you will search and filter on one of those platforms to find the Mercedes C class you want for the price you want to pay. But however likely that sounds it is not likely that this will happen. You now begin to wonder whether a Mercedes car is really what you want or you want to compare it to other cars in the same segment. Maybe you will start a new search like "BMW 3 series" or you search for "Top Gear blogs Mercedes C" if you want to read some reviews. The following day you may see the new Volvo S 60 wondering if that wouldn't be a good choice. And the search goes on and on. This may take days, weeks, months and even years. To tell you the truth, I am already searching for a new car although my current one is just a few years old (don't tell my wife please). I will not buy a new car for years to come but sometimes I cannot resist the search.

Another example: As I am writing this I just booked a rental car for our family holiday which starts in Las Vegas. What did I do? I started my search at the well-known car rental companies. I filtered it down to SUV's as that was my preselected choice of car and then I started comparing. Not much, because I hate comparing prices (I am that guy that always pays too much). Then I got back at Expedia where I had booked our flights and hotels and I started searching and filtering again. I saw a GMC SUV that looked all right and had the cargo space I needed for 4 large bags and hand luggage. Finally I booked this car. Did I stop there? No, in the evening I had second thoughts about the cargo space so I began searching again. I searched on Google images, YouTube and Google Search. I have seen a couple of videos and now I think I am all right. This is all after my booking and payment of the car. A bit too late? Maybe, but very normal human behavior called cognitive dissonance. And I now I will search again for this car when the holiday season is approaching.

What does that mean for our SEO strategy?

Okay, so our search habits are rather irrational. We skip back and forth form generic to specific and form logic to almost insane searches. For us SEO professionals this behavior has important implications. Let us explore the major ones:

1. Make room for generic search terms

I see a lot of SEO-ed websites that target lower-funnel keywords. Think of keyword combinations with "buy" or brandname + model + product type. There are no low or high funnel keywords so do not think that a keyword like this "buy new Nike Zoom Pegassus running shoes" should convert better than "Nike running shoes". So concentrate on these broader search themes, they are important. But, that doesn't mean we can forget about the specific ones.

2. Longer conversion paths, more & different touchpoints

As we are searching more and more, conversion paths will get longer. So in analyzing our statistics we will see more clicks (and even off line engagements) from different channels.
This is a classic conversion path:

Google Ads > Organic > Direct > ORDER

Looks very funnely, still occurs of course, but look at all other paths. You might see something like this:

Google Ads (2 times) > Direct > Organic > Google Ads > Organic (3 times) > ORDER

I come across conversion paths with no less than 80 to 100 clicks from a myriad of channels before someone finally orders. The major question is: Which channel has attributed most to our conversion? The answer: all of them. That makes it harder to pinpoint the most effective marketing strategy of course, but hard is good, that leaves enough opportunities for all market participants.

3. Forget last click conversion

The default conversion counter on most statistical packages including Analytics is last click conversion. The longer conversion paths tend to become the less sense this makes. But it never made sense. Why should that last click be more important than the earlier ones? So set your conversions to a more democratic engagement counter like Lineair or Time Decay. In this confusing no-funnel world we might even consider taking it a step further. Instead of measuring all our output by statistical conversions we might want to look at interactions and pageviews and REAL conversions. I know, I would prefer to know exactly what interaction at what time in someone's customer journey had the biggest impact on conversion. But if this is not measurable I am fooling myself by pretending I know.

4. Long copy for Long Tails

If you are an SEO consultant you know the discussion about short and long copy. In general long copy attracts more keyword combinations and especially long tail searches. It's just a matter of math, in long copy you automatically run a higher chance of making the perfect match with a search query. Writing longer copy is like playing the lotteries with more tickets, chances you win are higher. Consider all these back and forth searches, this zooming in and out. In order to do that people use longer and less logic search query's so concentrating on long tails makes pretty good sense.

5. You are not alone with your customer

We described the longer conversion paths that are part of this bigger picture of no-funnel search. These conversion paths consist of interactions with your website and your company. That is only part of the picture of course. The bulk of our target audience does not exclusively interact with us for that product or service we offer. We might get the order but take it from me, your customer has looked over the fence at your neighbor's offer. Between all the interactions with your website your customer has looked at other websites, blogs, the brand website, the website of the importer you are working with, Amazon, review sites and you name it. To understand this behavior is really important for our SEO strategy. Make sure that on all searches you offer the best possible information and make your offer visible and understandable. If you write that long copy about running shoes, make it authentic and try to connect to your audience with fine well written copy. Above all: Show what you have to offer without screaming for attention, most people are not ready yet to buy, but they like to see what you've got in store. It's like speed-dating a girl, this person that takes a seat at your table is interested in you. Tell her what she wants to know, make sure that you put on your brightest smile but don't ask her telephone number, yet... she will come back, maybe.

So, what to do?

- Think of touchpoints instead of a narrowing sales funnel.
- Understand that one single piece of website copy may attract people who will buy or people who orientate or compare.
- There is no general time table for search and convert. Some people will consider, compare,

reconsider and convert in 10 minutes, some will do the same in 5 months. So be sure that you always have a link or button to the actual commercial page like a sales page or lead generating page, also on your information pages. These pages may act as converting pages as people will skip your logical sales funnel process (it doesn't exist, remember).

- Make outstanding copy that will inform and induce action at the same time, it is up to the visitor to decide to become a customer or not but you may help him or her getting over the threshold.

Most important

Marketing is not about catching customers, it is about helping each single potential customer all along HIS or HERS individual path to our products or services.

17] Buying your way out

Total average SEO impact: ★★★

The impact of online advertising on SEO

Google always asserted that there is no direct link between using Google Ads and a better organic ranking on their search pages. They are right. Google is always right on most issues (this is a peculiar sentence I agree but I think it is the most accurate I can come up with). However, in an indirect way there is most certainly a link and it has implications on our SEO strategy.
Let us first discuss what the relation is between online advertising and SEO. It has several impacts and it is most distinctive with search ads. There is a relation with display ads or banners but this is not so profound as with Google or Bing search ads.

The relation between Search Ads and SEO

As you may have noticed I am talking about the relation between search ads and SEO. That is not the same as the relation between search ads and organic ranking although it is also intertwined. I will explore all relations.

1. Search advertising boosts organic traffic

This sounds like a direct link (which Google justly denies) but it is indirect. What happens when we start a Google Ads or Bing Ads search campaign? We will drive traffic to our website. A part of this traffic just don't like what we have to offer and it leaves us without ever coming back. Another part of this traffic likes what it sees or reads and is getting interested in what we have to offer whether that be our website content or the products or services we propose. There is a good chance that this piece of traffic will be searching for us again in the coming hours, days or even months. They may type in a search term that they think will bring them to our website or they will use our brand name, web domain or a combination with a search term. Maybe that will again trigger a Google or Bing Ad but in many cases people will be looking for the organic result (most people have the decency of not clicking on a paid ad when it is not needed, yes our human race is very empathic). When we will be looking at our Analytics data we will see organic growth. You might say that this organic growth is a bit artificial but that is only partially true.

2. Search engine advertising boosts organic ranking

Now we are talking! As people will use combinations of words that are relevant to our website in order to come back to us they will trigger search results within the SERP's that will bring them to our website. In some cases these search results will not be on position 1 but maybe on the lower part of the first page or even second page. As people click on lower ranking positions they essentially are voting them up. If this occurs in some volume (and I can tell you that these volumes need not to be too high depending on the niche you serve) we will see our rankings go up on these search terms.

3. Search ads do not suffice on longer conversion paths

As conversion paths tend to get longer and longer (people need more touchpoints in order to buy or leave a lead) people use different searches for the products we offer. In most conversion paths they will use a couple of combinations or Long Tails in their searching process. In most cases we will not be able to advertise on all these search terms as our budget will not allow that. Besides, your ad will not always be shown as Google is directing the process. A solid SEO strategy will help to catch these search queries, especially combinations and Long Tails. Moreover people specifically do not always click on ads. In about 70% of all searches they skip ads (or ads are not available) and they click on an organic search result. Research shows that people tend to click more on organic results when they are looking for information. That doesn't mean that they are not ready to buy. As we have discussed in this book, sales funnels are not linear, people may be ready to buy but just want to check on something. In many cases they use keyword combinations or Long Tail searches to get a more specific search result that will assist their buying process. If you would be able to come up on search results when your target audience is enquiring further information it will be a boost to your conversions. It will add relevance to your company and products and, more importantly, it will add authority. Is this always possible? No, of course not, it is impossible to always come above in search results on each and every keyword combination or Long Tail within your niche. But that doesn't mean we cannot enhance our results. So besides search advertising we must also add informative copy on our website. This can be done by adding generic information on product group of product category pages and adding the right and all-encompassing product specifications on our product or service pages. I can assure you that 90% of all online shops make a mediocre or even worse performance in that respect. The same goes for lead generating websites where you will find basic information about services or products offered but no in-depth information. By using Google Ads or Bing Ads they will be able to drive an interested potential customer to these pages but they fail to attract this same person when he or she is going down the path to conversion.

4. SEO does not suffice either

In my view you need both: a solid SEO strategy and a smart search advertising campaign. For my customers I use both Google Ads and Bing Ads but Google is my first pick as they are the dominant search engine in the countries I work for. Why can't you rely solely on organic traffic? The simple reason is that you will not be able to rank high on all important keywords and combinations (not even after you read this book, sorry). For small companies or independent entrepreneurs it may be an option but for medium sized and larger companies or online retailers who need a constant flow of orders living on organic traffic only will be hard. Besides, they would sell themselves short if they did not tap into the opportunities of search advertising. That is not the same as telling that you should go all-out on search advertising, on the contrary. I have access to Analytics data of hundreds of websites from all sorts of industries and all sorts of companies, small, medium-sized to very large. In general, this is what occurs on 90% of all these websites: Most of organic traffic comes in from 1 or 2 high volume and competitive single keywords and the bulk of all other organic traffic consists of specific keyword combinations and Long Tails. In most industries there are 5 to 25 relevant high volume keywords and of course a score of combinations and Long Tails. Without search advertising you will not trigger these search queries. Should you then go for all blank spots in your search advertising campaign? Not at all! Single out the most relevant and put your money where it has the best return. It is very dependent upon the industry and the company's mission and sales goals how to support your organic traffic with search ads or vice versa.

5. Search engine advertising is great but bears some risks

The other part of the spectrum, solely relying on search advertising is a mistake as well. I must confess that I have some customers that rely too much on search advertising. Returns are (still) good and when enough money is at hand you can grow quickly and even internationally. The problem is that in the long term this may risk your entire business if advertising is getting too expensive (CPC's have a strong tendency to go up during the years) or if product margins go down (the fierce competition is driving selling prices down, eroding margins). The highest risks run pure online players that have an aggressive growth strategy. They do not like to put resources in the tedious work of writing website content and putting time and efforts into SEO. Why should they? They can reap the sales of today with advertising while the seeds of a sound SEO strategy are still in the ground. My advice: Balance your short term and long term strategies. Your SEO strategy is a hedge to your online search advertising strategy.

So, what to do?

- Look at your conversion paths in Google Analytics and try to understand the relation between the different channels (organic, paid search, direct traffic and referrals). You will notice that they are intertwined. Leave one stepping stone out of the path and what would have happened to your conversion? Would it still be there?
- Look where your strongpoints are in your SEO strategy. Which keyword themes outperform, which lag behind? Think of opportunities where search advertising may complement your online marketing strategy.

- Use search engine advertising like Google Ads and Bing Ads on important keyword themes where your organic power is weak.
- Don't try to oversell your paid traffic. It's a mistake to press people in converting because you want a "bang for your money". Do not make a blinded landing page without navigation. Give them the opportunity to inform AND to buy or convert. If they do not want to make a decision right now let them come back. Show them your great website content. Again, look at conversion paths and notice that most of paid traffic is in the beginning of a customer journey. Think: Paid > Organic against Paid > Conversion!

Most important

Analyze your conversion paths and your ranking on search themes. Balance search engine advertising with your SEO strategy. Look at the total of your conversions, not at conversions per channel or you might be fooling yourself.

18] Across the border

Total average SEO impact: ★★★★★

How to set up an international SEO strategy?

International SEO is difficult, do not underestimate it. In fact, I sincerely believe that you must consider the help of our friends Google or Bing in using their advertising platforms. That being said, difficult is good, that means the threshold is higher for your competitors too. Adding to that, I serve a number of customers who made a serious impact with their international SEO strategy. So don't get too gloomy but know that there is work to be done.

What are the challenges of international SEO?

Let us explore some of the biggest ones:

1. Search engines prefer local websites

Search engines are becoming more and more regionally relevant. A search query coming from one country is matched with a search result coming from the same country. A search query that seems like a local one will trigger local search results, often based upon geo-targeting from mobile devices. There are two main reasons why search engines go local. The first is relevance. They think they better serve users with local results. The second is serving more relevant ads and broadening the scope of advertising. By going local they make search engine advertising more interesting for local advertisers enlarging their advertising market. This all sounds logic and okay but it hampers an international SEO strategy. You should beat relevance of local players. That notches up the bar for your international SEO efforts.

2. It will impact your complete website strategy

There are a number of things to consider. These involve selecting the right domain extension. Should you go for 1 domain and several language extensions such as www.example.com/fr (for french) and www.example.com/de (for german) or go all the way and choose www.example.fr and www.example.de?The former involves 1 website, the latter several different websites. You also may go for country subdomains such as www.uk.example.com and www.de.example.com. There are pros and cons for each and every option. Another question involves hosting. Ideally you should host a website targeting the USA within the USA and the best way to do that is by going for ccTLD's (country code top level domains). But when you opt for the best technical way in most cases you will end up with the option that requires the most time, energy and money. Will it all be worth it? That is one reason why some companies choose search engine advertising as their gateway to online export.

3. The language issue

Going across the border generally implies going to another language area. Not only will it impact your content strategy but also your lead generation process and ordering process. Products and instructions should be labelled in that particular language. More importantly, your back office should be able to speak that language, a challenge that is not always easy to meet. Add to that the SEO process which faces higher entry barriers with a new website or new content facing local contenders favored by search engines. In this environment you must produce better and more in-depth content than the existing contenders in that other language. Not a frivolous task.

Okay, so it's not easy, should I crawl back in my shell?

Of course not! I just want you to know it will take energy and time before you will see some results. Just start your SEO strategy and mix it with some smart online marketing stuff. What would I do? Below is a strategy that I am familiar with. It has worked for me and several of my customers.

Step 1: Determine your goal country

You need to make a choice about what country you will be targeting. Many considerations are involved here (competitive strength in that country, logistical issues, legal issues and size of market for instance). My advice: Pinpoint 1 country, do not go for more countries even if they speak the same language.

Step 2: Choose you technical strategy

Here issues like domains, separate website and hosting will be decided upon. Again, there are many choices to make. In general a separate website with a dedicated domain and local hosting may be the right choice from a purely SEO mindset. But there are more issues than SEO alone so think this true from all angles.

Step 3: Decide on your commercial content

What products and services will be proposed to that particular country? Maybe it will differ from your local proposition. When a decision is made, start writing hese commercial pages in that language.

Step 4: Establish a content strategy aimed at that country

How will you make a difference in website content? Here the SEO ball starts really rolling. I will always begin by making a concrete plan tackling chosen keyword themes and building URL structures. Sometimes I advise to begin with a specific theme that we start to cover completely and thoroughly. In other cases I advise to begin with the first layer of keyword themes in a more broader sense. For example, if you are a seller of high end leather accessories for women you could start with one particular very relevant keyword theme like "exclusive leather handbags" and make different pages around this specific theme. Another option is to begin with themes like "leather handbags", "leather purses" and "leather ladies belts" and then work your way down with in-depth keyword themes.

Step 5: Start a search advertising campaign on specific keywords

In almost all cases (well, just scrap the word almost) SEO will not suffice in the short term to get things moving. I do not like a wait-and-see strategy. I prefer action. In almost all cases (well, just scrap the word almost) my customers think likewise. To stir things up I would advise to use Google Ads or Bing Ads or any other search advertising platform to bring in the first orders and to study target group behavior. By doing that we will learn if our products or services will be met with enthusiasm or with total neglect. In either case we will learn valuable insights. Besides we will also test our order processing and logistics system selling to a new country. Another advantage, we will learn which specific keywords our target country uses. This is very, very, important! Due to language challenges we will almost always (well, just scrap the word almost) experience some missing keywords our new target group uses. You may use a professional translating agency but they will not be able to translate your specific products and services in all the possible words our potential customers use. Translators may not understand our products very thoroughly (especially in B2B markets operating in technical markets), besides they are used to come up with 1 or 2 translations while in practice there may be 10 synonyms for the products you want to move. It depends on the language how many variations there are of course. Some languages really are full of different words describing more or less the same products and services. By using search engine advertising we will learn synonyms if we us the right keyword type. I prefer phrase match to start such a campaign. It will trigger direct synonyms but not completely irrelevant words like broad match will deliver. By selecting broad match you will be overwhelmed by synonyms. I would try that after a few months. We can use the data for our SEO strategy.

Step 6: Reconsider the market

This may sound like a strange step. Why reconsider, we already have decided to go for that market? But it is wise to do. We have gathered extra information from our Google Ads or Bing Ads campaigns. We have witnessed our own order processing system in practice. Are we pleased with the outcome? If so, we can take it to another level. If not, better to pull the plug while it still doesn't hurt that much.

Step 7: Step up the SEO process

With insights form our first transactions or leads getting in and with the keyword data pouring in from search engine advertising we have more accurate ammunition to use in our SEO strategy. Now it is time to go full throttle in copywriting and publishing content. Of course it will take time so I advise to keep the search advertising campaign running until we have enough organic traffic to tune it down (or maybe keep it as it is if the ROI is positive).

So, what to do?

- Research opportunities and threads before you will dive into a new market abroad. Do not underestimate it, but don't be shy either.
- Set up an execution plan. Beware that SEO takes time to flourish and especially in another country and even more so in another language.
- Dedicate a team that will cover all content creation aimed at that specific country.
- You may want to translate existing content into this new language. That would be a time-saver but make sure your translation is right (especially in

technical markets). In most cases a 1 on 1 translation doesn't do the job.

- Mix SEO with search engine advertising and learn from the data!

Most important

Do not expect to make a success of it overnight. Count in years, not months. That goes for your SEO efforts as well as your complete international online strategy.
Act > Learn > Optimize > Improve > Analyze > Get into the details > Perfect > International growth realized > Get some sleep

19] Beware of bearded web designers

Total average SEO impact: ★★★★★

A new website that turns into a nightmare

Web designers love making new websites. If they would have it their way they would build a new website every 2 years. Creative destruction is what they really love. They like to start with a clean sheet. And who can blame them? Well, we SEO professionals can and we should. I have come across many new websites being built by ambitious web designers whose only focus is creativity and design. Before you think I have a grudge against web designers, I do not. On the contrary, I need them, but they need me too. I have to add that I know many web designers that know what they are doing and also understand that although beginning from scratch would be tempting it would not be wise.

So what's the problem?

There are web designers (the bad ones) that throw away all existing website content and especially website content that they believe is distracting website visitors from the main company mission, selling products and services. They prefer a clear-cut communication by as little words and as many graphics and visuals. In essence they hate copy, especially if it is long and explaining. That just doesn't fit their mindset of communicating with design. So what may happen? Someone in the company decides to build a new website for whatever reason (new design, new markets, new technical features). They hire a web designer. The web designer comes up with a sexy design. Everybody is thrilled with the proposal. The web designer finally (always later than expected) comes up with a brand new website (and yes, it is really brand new). The new website is going life, replacing the old one. Everybody happy. And then, after one month someone thinks, "hey, what happened to conversions and traffic?" And then they call you.

How wrong can it go?

Terribly. Web designers may make several mistakes that will lead to a drop in organic traffic. I have seen them all, unfortunately. Before I will get into these mistakes I want to stress the seriousness of the problem. I am not talking about a 5% drop in organic traffic whenever you put a new website in place of the old one. Such a drop is normal. In fact you will always lose organic traffic when you replace the old website with a new one. Even if all URL's remain exactly the same. I must confess that I do not know the exact reason for that, theoretically when all has proceeded according to plan there should not be a drop but it occurs almost always. The serious problem I am talking about is loosing 15% up to 70% of all organic traffic. This 70% unfortunately is more common than you would think. If you do not follow any of the SEO rules of putting a new website "live" in general you will loose 70% of organic traffic. And I have seen this happening a lot.

And how can it go wrong?

In many ways. Here are some typical reasons why your web designer may have f-ed up your online presence. I will talk about "he" referring to such a web designer which is not correct because I have met some female web designers who also messed things up. But somehow I have a particular persona in mind when I am talking about the over-creative, zealous web designer that is single-mindedly focused on artistical design (not technical design unfortunately). In my persona this web designer wears a too short T-shirt with some in-your-face remark on it, and is bearded of course. Again I have to add that whenever I met someone who resembled my persona he proved me wrong. So I really have to reconsider my persona but somehow it has stuck with me. Forgive me! So what may this "bearded" web designer have done?

1. He threw away all your SEO content

This happens more than you would think. Especially with online shops this is a real danger. Redesigning an online shop automatically focusses all attention on getting the products into your shop and simple written content is often overlooked. This is not always the fault of the design team of the web bureau. In most cases it is the technical designer that just forgot about migrating website content that does not include products and prices. It is a mindset thing, designers are too focused on getting the products into new pages that they overlook the SEO content.

2. He chose a new URL lay-out

Why changing existing URL's when it is not really necessary? Don't do it. Keep the existing URL's in place. It will make the migration process easier and the Google's of this world do not have to work their way through numerous redirects which will hamper your online presence anyway.

3. He forgot to redirect

O, o, this is a classic. And it happens so often. Whenever new URL's are put into use, please redirect the old ones and do it RIGHT AWAY! In many cases web designers forget about redirecting all together and when they think about it, it is often too late.

4. Finally we got rid of all that "bad" content

Another classic but we cannot blame the web designer completely on this one, although I think a good one should say: "sorry, but this is not a good idea". What happens? When the decision is being made about making a new website, the web designer asks whether all current content should be migrated. In many cases the client will get the instruction to go through all pages and inform the web designer about pages that do not need to go over to the new website. Then things go wrong. It's such fun striking out old content that some clients get hooked upon going for "new". When you have a "new" mindset all things old are obsolete, so let's get a fresh start. That feels right doesn't it? Yeah, but they forget the traffic that these pages attract from search engines. Even these old pages that do not fit the company's mission anymore may get in tons of traffic. Instead of writing them off you should rewrite them. Again, this doesn't fit very well in a process when a new website is being designed. Bothering your mind with old content just doesn't match with building a new website. But you really should! Before you want to get rid of an old webpage, look at your Analytics data. If it's an "engine page" (a web page that sucks in organic traffic): Do think twice, it's not all right!

5. Bye bye old images, time for something 3.0

The truly graphic web designer loves images and graphics. But not old ones. There is always a new design format, a new sexy way of building a website that makes all older designs soooooooo booooooring. There is only one solution: Get rid of it right away. Okay, these older images with those nice Alt Tags may come up at top spots in Google images, but who cares! Not your casually but cleverly dressed web designer. But I do. Image Search is important, especially for those among us who don't like reading and love images, like bearded web designers. Please incorporate these well-found old images in your new website. You may replace them to a dedicated page, although that bears some risks, but do not throw them away.

So, what to do?

1. Beware that a new website is by no means a win-win. It is a real challenge to keep the organic traffic stable after migration.
2. Make a migration plan. Get your SEO strategist on the table. Don't leave it all to the designer.
3. Is it really necessary to have a new website? Do you really think that this new design will drive sales? Do not chase every new styling craze, web design is not a fashion, it is a craft.

Most important

Cherish what you have. Do not throw away that what made your online success. A new website is fine, a completely new design is sometimes needed but that isn't the same as starting all over again. You can have both: a great new website, a modern design AND old website content that still drives organic traffic and sales. Don't settle for less!

20] Optimizing your Return On Perspiration

Total average SEO impact: ★★★★★

Getting the most out of your sweat

In essence Search Engine Optimization is free of charge. It only requires smart-thinking, concentration, writing and publishing. In practice it is a time consuming exercise that often leads to headaches and occasional spells of gazing out of the window related to temporary writer's blocks or plain blackouts. But on average it is all good fun. Really, it's a great job that so many people hate to do that they are glad to outsource it which makes my bread and butter. It is true, there are not many people that love the exercise of writing which is the essence of SEO. It doesn't come without effort and it creates sweat, sometimes the smelling one but always the exhausting one. That leaves us with one of the most important questions of this book: How can we make sure that we get the most out of our perspiration? In fact, in my day-to-day work as an SEO consultant I try to teach marketing teams to really make this their number 1 concern.

Motivation by results

Well performed SEO will drive in free and relevant traffic to a company's website. In this world of cut throat online competition where driving in traffic through advertising is getting more and more expensive every day SEO is number 1 on everybody's online marketing to-do list. That makes sense, but it is not true. In fact, it is way down on the bottom if it's on it at all. Why is that? For one thing: SEO takes time to get in the results. But this is not a valid argument as in most cases results can be picked up within 2 months (if your website/domain is not brand new). Another, more common reason, is that many marketing departments do not take time to monitor the results. They are not going through their Analytics in the right way or they have the wrong reports before them. Then there are numerous managers who don't believe in SEO. They either think that Google is so smart that you don't need to do your utmost to boost your organic traffic or they think that SEO is just a scam. So what do I do? I try to drive in organic traffic as fast as possible and I will show that their efforts really materialize by showing the right hard data. That will cause the mindshift I am after. For action motivation is always number 1. And the best motivation is fast results.

Going for the low hanging fruit

To drive in relevant organic traffic the fast way, we must look for search themes that are really relevant to our website. Search engines will understand these themes better and faster as relevance is clear. To come up with these themes I always start with a keyword research report. We need to know what keywords are relevant to our market. I always list them up by themes so we get an overview of keywords that makes sense, not a hotchpotch of unrelated keywords. Then it is time to take a look at our website. What keyword themes are really important to our specific product or service but are underexposed on our website? That is where you should start. These keyword themes should be as close as possible to what we are offering and here we must add theme-depth. With theme-depth I mean getting to the content bottom of a specific keyword theme. Let's say we are a local car rental firm in Houston Texas. Of course keyword themes involving "car rental" and "Houston" are extremely relevant. There are a lot of different keywords that include these subthemes but we can't trigger them all (otherwise we would be too manipulative for Google and friends). But we can do more than we might think using some creative thinking. We can add brands we rent and use the combination "Houston" and we can make pages that describe our location at the airport in Houston or describing how to get there from the airport and so on. These themes are the most low hanging fruit available. Just a bit higher in the tree are themes like "car rental near me" tapping into mobile search and "car rental" + "discounts" tapping into large search volumes and relying on local searches with that combination. We always must go up in the tree starting from the bottom. That is why it is called ORGANIC TRAFFIC, it grows slowly from root to top. In order to bear fruits we must fertilize it with our ideas and actions and then we can reap what we sow. It goes without saying that your back will hurt a little in the process.

10 steps to get fast SEO results

Let's make things more systematic. Whenever I consult marketing teams on SEO I promise them that results will come after their efforts. To fulfill these promises I use a chronological approach to fire-start the process. Here it is:

1. Start with a thorough keyword research

2. Arrange all keywords in broader keyword themes

3. Pick the keyword themes that are most relevant to the market and existing website

4. Choose the specific keywords within each theme as new pages to write

5. Make a hierarchical URL cluster for each keyword theme

6. Decide on specific URL's and make a graphic structure how pages are linked

7. Decide on SERP title and meta description

8. Determine the topics you will cover for each new webpage

9. Start writing

10. Publish your webpage (and don't forget to put in a Call to Action)

This approach will work. The most important steps are 3 + 4 + 5 + 9. We already talked about step 3 and 4. With step 5 we will add the logic that search engines love. If one of our keyword themes would be "**Houston car rental**" we may find the following keywords as relevant:

houston car rental
houston car rentals cheap
houston car rental exotic
houston car rental luxury
houston classic car rental
houston sports car rental
Then there may be separate keyword themes that will add relevance to the above mentioned themes such as the theme **rentals by car make** with separate keywords like:
Ford Fiesta car rental
Jeep Cherokee car rental
Ford Mustang Cabrio car rental
Lamborghini car rental
Porsche car rental
Rolls Royce wedding car rental

We can add logic by using a simple hierarchical structure that may look like:

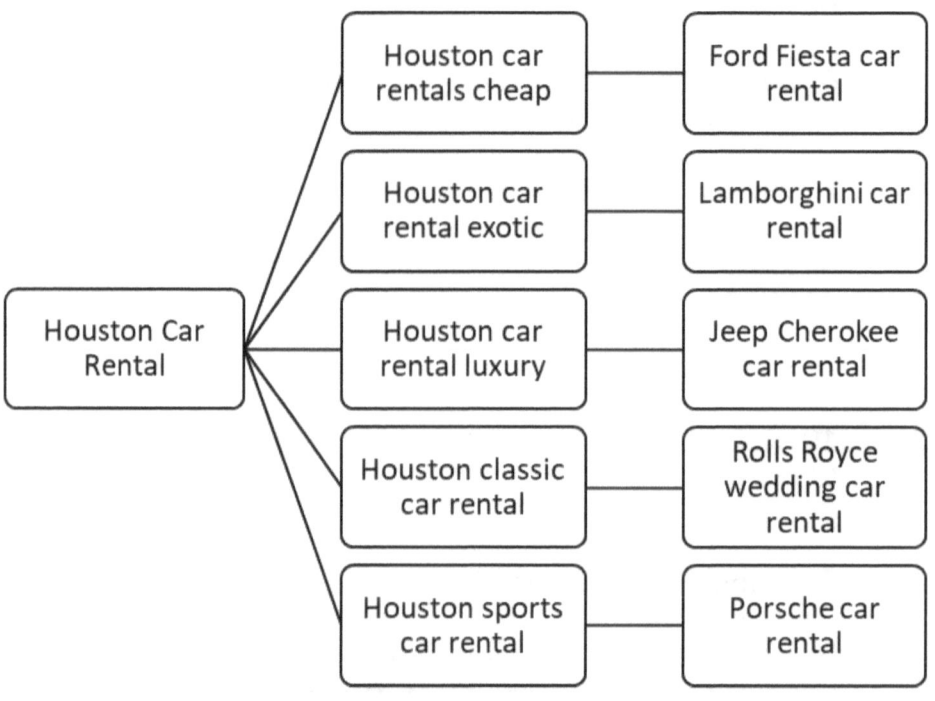

This will give us the basis for our webpages and URL structure. Our webpages and URL's may look something like this:

www.example.com/houston-car-rental
www.example.com/houston-car-rental/houston-car-rentals-cheap
www.example.com/houston-car-rental/houston-car-rentals-cheap/ford-fiesta-car-rental-houston
www.example.com/houston-car-rental/houston-car-rentals-exotic
www.example.com/houston-car-rental/houston-car-rentals-exotic/lamborghini-car-rental-houston
www.example.com/houston-car-rental/houston-car-rentals-luxury
www.example.com/houston-car-rental/houston-car-rentals-luxury/jeep-cherokee-car-rental-houston
www.example.com/houston-car-rental/houston-classic-car-rental
www.example.com/houston-car-rental/houston-classic-car-rental/rolls-royce-wedding-car-rental-houston
www.example.com/houston-car-rental/houston-sports-car-rental
www.example.com/houston-car-rental/houston-sports-car-rental/porsche-car-rental-houston

Of course we can make other breakdown URL structures from our keyword themes. What's important is the logical interdependence between linked pages and the hierarchy (broad comes before specific).
If you will follow the above mentioned steps I guarantee you that you will get the fastest results possible. But how fast and what search volumes you will trigger depends upon some important issues like:

1. The seniority and health of your domain

Search engines love websites that are proven. They prefer older ones they can trust and they do not want to be manipulated which also benefits established domains and websites. Yes my friends, Google appreciates the stability and steadiness that comes with old age.

2. The competitiveness of your market niche

Do not think you can squeeze your website into the top spots of a highly competitive niche overnight. It takes more time the more webpages compete for the same keywords. But do not be intimidated about that. Within time you can beat them all.

3. Your copywriting ability

Your webpage content should be brilliant. It must be specific, relevant and adding value to the people behind the search query (never forget that there is a real person behind each and every query). The most important difference between poor and brilliant content is the value it will offer to your target audience. Say it straight, give all you've got and approach your subject from all angles. And never forget: write in an original and personal style.

4. A little bit of luck

Hope is never a good strategy but when you do everything right luck may help you. What am I talking about? Surely, you don't want to hear that all depends on luck. Well, it doesn't. But when you write 10 superbly written articles, do everything right on a technical level and follow all necessary steps you will notice that not all of these 10 published webpages will score as high as you wanted on search engine results pages. Sometimes search engines just do not pick up your content like you might hope. Do not get bothered by that, it happens to all of us. You may call this bad luck but as I am a positive guy I turn it around and tell you that when you do a brilliant job Mr. Luck will push it further than you expected. But cut him some slack, sometimes he takes a break, you do too.

Look at the results, and keep looking!

Do your SEO efforts lead to something? Yes, if you do it right. But what are we after? In most cases we want a rise in organic traffic. Well, we want more, we want a rise in relevant organic traffic. And in most cases we want this new traffic deliver conversions whether it be leads, subscriptions or hard online orders. I miss something you might think. What about ranking? Don't we want our webpages to rank higher on certain keywords? I can say it to you plain and simple: I don't give a heck about rankings. They are too difficult to gauge in an objective manner. And why should I focus all my attention on a bunch of single keywords as the bulk of the traffic and the most relevant traffic is in the long tails? Forget about rankings. I know your client or manager may be interested in them but it is up to you to explain they are chasing ghosts. Okay, but where to look for this rise in organic traffic? Google Analytics will do just fine. Go to your channel metrics and dig into the organic channel. How is the traffic volume evolving over time? That is my first question. Second is how each and every webpage is contributing. Here I am looking for what I call my engine pages, the ones that trigger organic traffic. Look for the new webpages you have published in the last 6 months and see how they drive in traffic (or not). But there is something you must reckon with. Even if your webpage contributes to the overall volume of organic traffic it sometimes doesn't show up in your list of webpages that trigger organic traffic. In a number of cases Google and other search engines supply the Homepage on their SERP's although another webpage contributes to the relevance. This doesn't sound logic but it happens. Search engines often show people the front door of your website even if it was one of your deep cellar pages that matches the search query and was responsible for showing this result. This may occur more with webpages that are relatively older.

In general it works like this:

1. A new webpage will begin showing organic results within 2 months after publication (in general, when all is done well and the requirements are met like we discussed here above).

2. This webpage will show up in your Analytics report under destination URL's within the organic channel metric.

3. This webpage is gaining more and more momentum in the period of 2 months between 36 months after publication as it will trigger more long tails and even some important combinations or single keywords.

4. After 36 months the volume remains stable.

5. As this webpage has built up relevance on some keywords or combinations it will spread this relevance over the complete website (not in an even way but it will spill over relevance to other pages).

6. Search engines may now decide to show the Homepage instead of the webpage it started the relevance. It depends on the search query whether they will do this or not.

You will have to look at your results with the above in mind. Most important however is to look, think and report the results. Motivation will follow. And this is what we are after. We want to show the results of our perspiration in order to fire start a continuing process of smart content building.

So, what to do?

- Start with your list of keywords and put them in a thematic order.
- Select those keyword themes and keywords that are most related to your proposition and existing website content.
- Write with a heart for customers and a mind for search engines.
- Keep track of the results and be sure to distribute them among the ones that decide upon budgets and time allocations (management) and all people who are actually doing the nitty gritty work of writing and publishing.

Most important

The number 1 rule for effective SEO: Analyze – Think – Write – Add value – Add logic – Analyze – Report – Motivate – KEEP UP THE GOOD WORK!

A last say about SEO

Whatever you will be hearing in the coming 10 years, SEO is here to stay. You will hear from new marketing gurus that will tell you that search engines are now so smart that SEO has become obsolete. You will be hearing from tech geeks that content does not matter anymore. And you will hear from self-called experts that voice search is now so dominating that written content is a thing from the past. They will all be wrong. That sounds a bit know-it-all arrogant from me, doesn't it? I guess that's right. But I dare to make that claim. Why? Because SEO is not a tricky, corner cutting, going for the quick win strategy. It is a way of helping search engines better understand your website content. More importantly, it is intended to inform people, to come up with the best possible answer on their questions. When people are truly interested in something they will search through some kind of search engine and they will take their time reading what triggers their interest. Voice search will become more important but search engines only supply answers from the best possible content written.

It's all about helping

Search Engine Optimization is not a selfish tactic. It's aimed at helping your target audience with the best possible answers to their questions and helping search engines to do their work more easily and rapidly. Besides the tactics mentioned in this book there are 2 basic rules of SEO. All tactics you read here or elsewhere are influenced by one single DO and one single DON'T.

So for all you guys and girls who want to look at SEO from a more broader perspective, this is what you need to do and stop doing:

1. Do be relevant
2. Don't be manipulative

Be relevant to your potential customer, be relevant to anyone who is interested in what you have to offer. Give them all information and insights you can come up with. Be honest, be straightforward, be helpful. Search engines are there to help making the match between questions and answers. They are your friends, you should treat them likewise. Don't fall for the trap of taking without giving. Don't go for short cuts, don't try to outsmart them. That is not the way to make friends and establish a long time relationship.

Ask not what your search engine can do for you, ask what you can do for your search engine!

I hope this book was also helpful for you. That was the reason of writing it. If you have further questions you can get in touch with me through LinkedIn.
Before I forget it: If you liked what you read, please leave a review. I would appreciate it very much. If you didn't like it, well, eh, show some compassion please.

I wish you all the best in your SEO strategy.

Paul Haarman, Breda, The Netherlands, 2019